Lloyd Sederer, MD, is an adjunct professor at the Columbia University School of Public Health.

In 2013, Dr. Sederer was given the Irma Bland Award for Excellence in Teaching Residents by the American Psychiatric Association, which in 2009 had recognized him as the Psychiatric Administrator of the Year. He has been awarded a Scholar-in-Residence grant by the Rockefeller Foundation and an Exemplary Psychiatrist Award from the National Alliance on Mental Illness (NAMI). In 2019, he received the Doctor of the Year award from The National Council on Behavioral Healthcare (representing over 3,000 mental health, addiction, and social service organizations serving over 10 million patients).

He has published seven books for professional audiences and, with this book, six for lay audiences, as well as 500 articles in medical journals, non-medical publications, and book, film, TV, and theatre reviews. His writings have appeared in The New York Times / International Herald Tribune, The Atlantic, The Wall Street Journal, The NY Daily News, The Washington Post, The Boston Business Journal, Commonweal Magazine, and Psychology Today, among other publications. He was, for 7 years, the medical editor for Mental Health for the HuffPost, where over 250 of his posts and videos appeared. He also wrote a regular opinion column on mental health and the addictions for US News & World Report. He has taught medical writing for the lay public at Columbia Medical School for 18 sequential semesters.

For my family, in the hope I have honorably portrayed them

and

for Bill Zinsser.

Lloyd Sederer

INK-STAINED FOR LIFE

Coming of Age in the 1950s, A Bronx Tale

AUSTIN MACAULEY PUBLISHERS™

LONDON • CAMBRIDGE • NEW YORK • SHARJAH

Ordering Information:
Quantity sales: special discounts are available on quantity purchases by corporations, associations, and others. For details, contact the publisher at the address below.

Publisher's Cataloging-in-Publication data
Sederer, Lloyd
Ink-Stained for Life

ISBN 9781645757702 (Paperback)
ISBN 9781645757719 (Hardback)
ISBN 9781645757726 (ePub e-book)

www.austinmacauley.com/us

Library of Congress Control Number: 2020938329

First Published (2020)
Austin Macauley Publishers LLC
40 Wall Street, 28th Floor
New York, NY 10005
USA

mail-usa@austinmacauley.com
+1 (646) 5125767

"Learning and laughter are two of my favorite things. Because they are much needed in these times. Dr. Sederer achieves both in this humorous yet telling side of New York, as he brings you back in his time machine – one built by a shrink!

As a New Yorker, fellow psychiatrist, and parent, reading his book revealed the childhood roots of a successful and prominent physician and friend, and an era that shaped our country. This book is a delight for all."

— Sue Varma, MD, PC, DFAPA
Board Certified Psychiatrist, Television Contributor,
Clinical Assistant Professor, NYU Langone

*****

"What makes a life? In particular, what makes a life, well-lived, in the service of others? Dr. Lloyd Sederer artfully tells the story of *his* life, from his humble beginnings in the Bronx to becoming one of the most influential psychiatrists in the country. But in telling his story, he teaches us how one weaves the fabric of a life from the good fortune of what we are given, together with the hard work that creates excellence. He shows us how we are shaped by the world around us, but also how we can, if we apply ourselves to it, also shape that world, leaving it better for the next generation. It is a privilege to be allowed this view into Dr. Sederer's journey, one we can all learn from."

— Sandro Galea, MD, DrPH
Dean & Knox Professor, Boston University School of
Public Health

*****

"Rarely do we get to peek into the childhood years of a person who later in life became a friend or a colleague. Here we have a tightly packed account of boyhood experiences that, by some unforeseen but delightful happenchance, shaped Lloyd Sederer's future as an eminent psychiatrist, public servant, author, and critic. You will find among these inspiring pages the stepping stones that led to his being a catalyst for a better world and, also for many, a damn good friend."

— Msgr. Donald Sakano
Priest of the Archdiocese of New York

*****

"Lloyd Sederer has found the pulse of memoir—that it is a life story, studded with indelible vignettes. More deeply, it is a spirited meditation on that life and its times. Read *Ink-Stained for Life* and you are in the Bronx of 50, even 60 years ago, feeling the imprint of immigration and assimilation. You also are in the mind of a dedicated physician who is surveying more than his New York boyhood. In this narrative, Sederer achieves an arc of values and beliefs, something like the rainbow that surprises him on a harrowing trek at the end of the book, what Keats called 'a vale of soul-making.'"

— Patricia Hampl
Internationally recognized memoirist, whose most recent book is *The Art of the Wasted Day*

*****

"One of the nation's leading psychiatrists as well as a top-notch film-and-book reviewer and afficionados of the life intellectual opens up his early years to us in this engaging, beautifully rendered memoir. His stories and words have immense beauty and soul. This is a gem of a book. Highly recommended!"

— Edward Hallowell, MD
Author of memoir *Because I Come from a Crazy Family* and #1 NYT bestseller *Driven to Distraction*

*****

"How can we live our lives with meaning, success, and satisfaction? What mark will we leave?

Renowned psychiatrist Dr. Lloyd Sederer takes us deep into his life and development. What's unusual about this book is how helpful it is for understanding our own narrative and upbringing, almost egging us on to dive more deeply as we seek to understand ourselves. It's a gem of a book for anyone trying to understand family and purpose."

— Drew Ramsey, MD
Assistant Clinical Professor of Psychiatry, Columbia University, Author of *Eat Complete* (2016) and *Eat to Beat Depression and Anxiety: Nourish Your Way to Better Mental Health* (out 2021).

*****

"Lloyd Sederer MD has written a memoir in fourteen chapters, with added essays that relate each story to current concerns. As with Dr. Sederer's other books, I enjoyed it, especially the thread of Bronx-raised ambitious, Jewish boys who were told to *dress British, think Yiddish,* as well as to marry a shikse, satisfy their mother (become a doctor), and satisfy their father (make money but don't entirely reject being a Jew). And, yet, as Dr. Sederer bravely reveals in his conclusion, there is an Eastern European sadness, melancholy, dissatisfaction in this success.

'What does Faith mean?' he [Dr. Sederer] asks himself in his last chapter. For him, it is not that everything is organized somehow with you in mind. Being a Jew can be humble as well as arrogant, an inferiority complex wrapped in a superiority complex, as Sederer in his newest book shows us. He has the right, the duty, of rejecting G-D, though not a Higher Power. This means that he is stuck with a universe that is oh so beautiful but leaves him rather out of sorts."

— Victoria Sweet, MD
Prize-winning author of *God's Hotel* and *Slow Medicine*

*****

"Lloyd Sederer takes us on a wonderful nostalgic ride through New York in the 1950s and into the 1960s, weaving his personal family narrative against the story of upwardly mobile immigrants, all seen through his discerning psychological lens. I found in his story so many common reference points that resonated and enriched my own memories of growing up in New York. I highly recommend this exceptional memoir that brings to life so many cultural milestones that we all share."

— Francis Greenburger
Chairman and CEO of Time Equities, Inc.;
Chairman and Founder, Greenburger Center for Social and Criminal Justice

*****

"A marvelous memoir filled with wisdom that elevates humanity! Dr. Lloyd Sederer is a public health hero. He has modeled a life of contribution in medicine, public service, and social justice. Fourteen illuminating stories, in Sederer's graceful and compassionate prose, inspire us to strive to make the world a better place and focus on what matters most—our fellow human beings."

— Kelli Harding, MD, MPH
— Author of *The Rabbit Effect*, Assistant Clinical Professor of Psychiatry, Columbia University, Irving Medical Center

*****

"Lloyd Sederer's *Ink-Stained for Life* offers a precious window into the lived experiences and meaning-making journey of one of New York's (and beyond) most treasured and impactful psychiatrists. Albert Schweitzer once said, 'My life is my argument.' Lloyd demonstrates in this beautiful memoir that his life is his argument. Filled with 14 stories from his boyhood, each matched with an essay relating it to our present world, and written with grace and humility, he helps us see the beauty and adventure that lies in building a life in service to others."

— Angela Coombs, MD
Clinical Instructor in Psychiatry at Columbia and Attending Psychiatrist in a public program serving younger adults with serious mental illnesses.

Table of Contents

Author's Note

It is a long drive from New York City to Albany, NY, the state's capital—and back—where my "official" office had been located. I have gone there a lot. When not on phone calls or listening to NPR (transfixed by dreaded further news about our federal government or the climate), I turn to audiobooks.

On the CD I was playing returning from Albany to the City on a sunlit day not long ago, I heard the warm yet cranky Yankee voice of my favorite writing teacher, Bill Zinsser, now deceased. I had again listened to disc one *On Writing Well* but now moved on to the next two, which were about writing a memoir. I had no plan to write a memoir, not then, but I wanted to keep listening to Zinsser. I finished the two discs on memoir, which he had condensed from his books on that subject. He narrated the audio with characteristic "clarity, simplicity, brevity, and humanity," his core principles for writing. The discs, and his counsel, was over by the time I pulled up to my apartment in NYC.

What stuck in my mind was his method for writing a memoir. Stick to a specific time and place, he urged. Be sure you meet those two, clear coordinates you had chosen. Like Frank McCourt did in *Angela's Ashes*, or Jill Ker Conway did in *The Road to Coorain,* or Alfred Kazin did in *A Walker in the City*. Then sit down and write something, whatever your mind goes to that day, and do so the next day, the next, and so forth. Until you had not just a mound of material, but you had given life to the people who inhabited that same time and place with you, the feelings you had, any swirl of thoughts you recalled, as well as the sights, sounds and smells that would recreate your world on paper.

A couple of days later, the weekend arrived. I did as Zinsser instructed. I knew I had to start with growing up in the Bronx: I began from the time I could recall, which was from when I was about seven until I graduated from high school, ten years later. I drafted the 14 stories you will see. Then I realized they needed an "overcoat"—for each to be bundled with an essay that offered context and meaning. What more could be said about the story's theme, historical and cultural moments, as well as offer reflections on its message?

When I was five, my family had moved from the South Bronx to its northeast section, where Italians, Irish, and Jews lived in red-brick, mostly attached, modest three-decker, two-family homes, with tiny lawns in the back and single car driveways in the front. Small apartment buildings were intermixed along the chains of houses. Buses ran on most of the large streets, and the nearby Gun Hill Road subway station was above ground.

That was the 1950s, mostly, my coming of age—a time when my country also was coming of age. Having put the war behind it, America was starting to grow and prosper. Eisenhower was the President, the economy was taking off, there were not just jobs—there was *opportunity*.

Not for everyone, of course, and not everywhere. There was plenty of poverty and family pain throughout the city, and of course around the country and globe: people, adults, and children, who did not know where their next meal would come from or could depend on safety and stability in their housing. Children whose families were beset by domestic violence, which we know now lays down the neural pathways of trauma in their young brains. Families with active serious mental illness or alcoholism and drug dependence. These problems have not gone away, and their tragic stories fill the news, every day. I was a fortunate one, not riddled by these disruptors, and could go on with building a life.

In New York City, when I was a boy, if you were spared the social conditions that could kill souls, and were white (or Asian), a child of first or second-generation immigrants, meritocracy mostly prevailed, even for girls (up to college). You did not have to be born sipping from a silver spoon, but it might help. Public schools did not need metal detectors because no one carried a weapon. The only drugs around were cigarettes and beer. And education was pretty good, especially if you were diligent like my parents insisted I be.

Blacks and Hispanics (and first-generation immigrants) were not so lucky; they still must fight to realize their rightful place in our society. But I was white, Jewish, and from a family that prized education, even though no one had graduated college until I did. While there were basically no books in my home, except those my sister and I brought from school or the library, my parents had bought the full set of the Encyclopedia Britannica, which sat alone in a two-shelf, wooden bookcase at the top of the stairs, its golden spines alphabetically revealing roadmaps to knowledge.

The stories that emerged onto paper over the weeks after I listened to Zinsser are all here. Their common thread is that assimilation and success, in work and life, were within reach for my family and me. Not a log cabin story, but advancement was not going to be handed to me either. There were many prejudices back then: anti-Semites, racial injustices, private school quotas, and the like. But a good future was possible—if I tried hard, didn't give up, and made accomplishments in school the ticket to my future.

I was as neurotic as could be, full of self-doubt, and shy. I was no sports star either. In other words, I was just like most every other kid around me (though I didn't know that then). There were no family members who modeled a profession, nor any athletes. When I got really good grades or high scores on standardized city-wide exams, more doors opened, and I didn't screw up enough to foreclose going through them. When I stumbled, too many times to disclose, I picked myself up and kept going. No one was going to dust me off, say encouraging words or help me, there was just me. That was just how it was, and I knew no different.

I had some really good teachers, who showed me that being smart and kind was a good thing. My parents expected me to be a good student, so I was always acquitting myself by displaying evidence of excellence. My family had its share of tumult, but we were intact and upwardly mobile. The rest was up to me.

New York City today is very different from 60+ years ago. While it is more racially integrated, the public schools have suffered. Education is not reliably delivered, opportunity evanescent. Competition, if possible, may be greater, fostered by pricey tutors and prep exams, or maybe just more ruthless. The gap between the rich and the poor has vastly widened. Racial disparities in education, health, and work persist. Immigrants, especially now from Middle-Eastern countries, have it very hard, as xenophobia, even in New York, has come out of its dark recesses. Finding an affordable place to live, in *any* borough, rivals San Francisco. At least the air and the water are good.

I am fortunate to be a product of the 1950s, to have had a nuclear family that cared about each other, grandparents, aunts, uncles, and cousins, some of whom you will meet in the pages ahead. But to paraphrase, I was not born on third base. I made a life in the Bronx until I went to college, which is the time and place this memoir of stories and essays comes to an end.

*****

Precis

I can't say my growing up in New York City in the 1950s was in any way exceptional. Except in the ways that each person's life is unique, marked by its own peculiarities, embedded in a one-of-a-kind family, occasioned by circumstances made or happenstance, set in a particular period and place, and subject to the passage of time and the metamorphosis that no one escapes.

I was born on Victory in Europe (VE) Day, May 15, 1945, a moment when most of the world breathed a huge sigh of relief as the Germans and their Axis European allies unconditionally surrendered. World War II was not over, that would take a nuclear holocaust in Hiroshima and Nagasaki for it to finally conclude. I would live in a country no longer at risk of fascist rule and in a time when America would burst forward in its pride and productivity. The USA was now the leader of the "free world" and a land of immense potential for returning GIs and their families, for invention and innovation, the assimilation of diverse groups of immigrants, and corporate growth. Opportunities seemed unlimited, for many—but far from all. Racism and class distinctions still prevailed. America was an enterprising society that more than ever before would offer education and vocation. The conditions were there for creating a meritocracy.

My birthplace was the Bronx, the borough of New York City that sits atop legendary Manhattan, the latter known to some as the center of the universe. Myopic no doubt, especially if you land there from Mars. The Bronx, then, was no Manhattan, with no Wall Street, Greenwich Village, Chinatown, the Upper West or East Sides, or Harlem. But Manhattan was not the only borough with grand parks; the Bronx and Brooklyn had their share. Maybe Queens and Staten Island too, but they were like distant states to me. Despite being a Bronx boy, Manhattan soon was on the map of my life, a short pilgrimage away as some of the stories ahead will tell.

My parents were first-generation Americans. Their parents had immigrated from Eastern Europe, the Ukraine and Austro-Hungary, to flee anti-Semitic persecution and to seek a better future for their children, their most precious commodity, despite the toil and cost it would demand.

As a family, we first lived on Fox Street, in the South Bronx, in a tenement across the street from the corner grocery my father's parents owned and ran, along with my parents. I guess that would be a bodega today. I was cared for by my father's mother and my own, who took turns at the store and with me (and then my sister). By the time I was five, my indulged life was seriously truncated: my grandparents had died, my sister was born to steal way my exclusive pampering, and my father sold the grocery store. The neighborhood had become no longer welcome for white people like us, middle-class shop owners. Remember, Spike Lee's film, *Do the Right Thing*?

We moved to Eastchester Road, in the Northeast Bronx, a broad street of apartments and attached pre-war, brick three-decker homes. It ran perpendicular to Pelham Parkway, where the rich people lived—except they were not really rich, just a lot more prosperous than we were. My mother's parents, Rose and JT, lived in our home's street-level apartment, a separate unit but not at all separate in our lives as a three-generational family of six. Not done with the grocery business, my father used the proceeds from the sale of the Fox Street store to buy a small supermarket in Northern Manhattan, on Dyckman Street. *Lloyd's Supermarket*, he named it, I can only imagine as a gift to my mother. He hardly spoke to me, but he readily yielded to my mother on all matters about the children.

It was from the Eastchester Road home that I went to elementary school (P.S. 121), walkable by the time I was seven. P.S., as you likely imagine, stands for Public School; my entire education has been in public schools, including a state-run medical school and residency training program. After the sixth grade, as a boy entering the mental and physical tumult of adolescence, I went to P.S. 113, off Gun Hill Road, getting there by foot and bus, for what was then called Junior High School (JHS), grades 7–9. I was able to do the three grades in two years in a program called the "*SPs*" (Special Progress, one class with the same kids for both years, kept pretty separate from the rest of the rough and tumble of local Bronx students). I had no idea I would be admitted to the SPs; there was no entrance exam, though I dimly remember taking standardized exams in elementary school. I didn't know about the SPs, so when I was accepted into one, there was little to celebrate; conversely, I suppose,

I wouldn't have been disappointed if I were not. No one I knew prepped or was tutored for the city's standardized exams. It's not like that today, with school selection and qualifying test performance an overriding concern for youth growing up and their families. But, back then, I just stumbled ahead into JHS and the SPs. I was a lucky one.

Then after JHS, to my utter surprise (not kidding here), I was admitted to the Bronx High School of Science, also by scores on exams I had no clue about. At first, I informed my parents I would not go there, preferring instead to go to Evander Childs High School, down the hill from P.S. 113, where some of my friends would be going. But my friendships were limited, since my best friends were my cousins in Queens, so that reason soon lost credibility. My parents wisely did not debate my first response to not accept admission at Science, which surely would have hardened it. They allowed me the time to realize I might actually want to go to Science, because I liked school and was used to an accelerated program and smart kids. Science took two buses and a fair amount of foot travel to reach, but that was time for more day-dreaming on the way.

In 1962, I graduated from high school, which is when this memoir, and its fellow essays, come to an end. What was to come of my life, I would have to live to comprehend because I had not a clue. I was simply following the "get an education" path, as was the ethos of my culture. It's been a good run, for the most part. Full of schooling, friends, love and marriages, sports, disappointments and losses, moves around the eastern US, and one son and one step-son (and thanks to them, three very lively and lovable grandchildren) as well as an abundance of confusion, some hard-won measure of clarity, and ever-growing gratitude.

*****

Chapter 1
Ink-Stained for Life

Early on weekend mornings when I was eight, my father would shake me out of the kind of deep sleep only children seem to enjoy, to get dressed and drive with him from the Bronx to the suburbs to work in the stationery store that the family owned.

I could find no escape. Some mitigation arrived after a few hours of tiresome tasks in the form of a runny bacon-and-egg sandwich from a nearby deli, washed down with cold orange juice.

My first task on those Saturday and Sunday mornings was to put together The New York Times, Daily News, and Herald Tribune for the customers who started streaming in at about 8 am.

Saturday wasn't too bad since it was mostly a matter of unpacking the bundles that had been hurled into the store doorway from a passing truck. But Sunday was an ordeal. As many as ten weekend sections had to be lined up on a make-shift counter, put inside one another, stacked, and moved to the front of the store.

Newspapers are dirty things, with ink that finds its way onto your hands, face, and clothes. The magazine, the business and travel sections, the Week in Review, sports, and all those ads rubbed off on me, in more ways than one, at that Westchester stationery store across from the train depot (the business was called Depot Stationers).

My younger sister got to stay at home with my mother, showing up much later, maybe bringing lunch. I would also imagine the boys in the rich neighborhoods that surrounded the station, watching cartoons and on a course to a good life, while I was destined to put together the papers.

After the papers were done, there were the floors to be swept, shelves to be dusted, and inventory to be stocked. When I was ten, I graduated to the cash register but only after the chores were finished. I could add items in my head quickly and accurately, and some customers would marvel at my skill. A New York Times, Daily News, a magazine, two birthday cards, a pack of cigarettes, and some gum easy: That'll be $2.85.

On my breaks, which meant when no one was waiting or my father was not watching, I read comic books. The adventure heroes Superman, Superboy, Batman, and Robin transported me to worlds far from what I regarded as my Dickensian circumstances.

My father's relentless determination derived from the Great Depression and its awful deprivations and desperation, though I could only see it as ruining my weekends.

By the time I was a teenager, the business had grown into an office supply store, then a good-sized company.

My father, to my great surprise, did not expect me to carry on the family enterprise. He found summer work for me in a start-up business machine company in Lower Manhattan.

So began my exit not only from Depot Stationers but from my family as well. I was freed of weekend work and could sleep in and hang around.

But something had happened to me. I couldn't sleep as restfully, nor just do nothing. Instead, I would dribble a basketball to the playground a mile away from my home and shoot hoops for hours, perfecting my shot and trying to get into pickup games with boys who wanted someone bigger and better than me, too often breaking my glasses in a game, to my mother's chagrin.

I would read books about science or science fiction. I would work on projects from school, doing more than needed to be done. I took my cash register-honed math skills into poker games with high school friends, not doing too badly on most evenings. I had what in Yiddish is known as the *spilches*, or ants in my pants, a restlessness that needed to be satisfied by activity, or, God forbid, work.

Decades later, while the activities have changed, my being programmed for work has not. If anything, it has grown. I suppose success has reinforced it, but that has come too arduously and incrementally over a long period of time to account for my behavior.

The constant seems to be the bone-deep need to get up and work. That is what I am doing this Sunday morning. But instead of assembling papers, I'm writing for one.

*****

*****

1A: Work

Not so long ago, vast numbers of people in all nations, including my own, needed to work. Not for meaning or purpose or other such noble life goals, but to feed, house, and clothe themselves and their families. Besides, no higher purposes can be realized if hungry, cold, or homeless, as the great writer, Knut Hamsun, a Norwegian who was part of an early, growing oeuvre of psychological fiction, made painfully clear in his novel, *Hunger* (1890).

Most people in my country continue to need to work for sustenance and safety, far more if we look globally. But now, for many, their jobs are in peril, especially in developed nations. Do you know what is the most common job in the United States? If you guessed being a driver, you guessed right. Taxi, Uber/Lyft, truck, bus, train, plane, etc. But driverless vehicles will soon displace drivers.

The horizon is rapidly approaching for vehicles driven by computers and for drones delivering all forms of goods. Airplanes will be piloted from bunkers in the American South or West (until they too move to South Asia or Eastern Europe), with perhaps one warm-blooded pilot in the cockpit for show, to quell the anxieties of passengers seeing no one in the fore cabin.

Robots will (already have) dramatically reduced manufacturing and labor jobs, even the care and company of the elderly and infirm. Teachers, academic and trade, are being replaced by on-line courses and distance-learning programs, guaranteeing the ability to study and obtain credentials and skills when and where you want, for far less money (and time) than attending brick and mortar institutions with live bodies standing in front of the blackboard or lectern.

What will all these people do for work, to occupy their minds and lives? To earn a living? What will become of factory and assembly line workers, coal miners, teachers, drivers, delivery men and women, home health aides, even doctors and nurses?

In 2017, the government of Finland began a social experiment in which 2,000 unemployed adults, ages 25–58, were paid a "basic income" (~ $685/month), hoping this support would foster their re-employment, and add cash to a struggling economy. The plan was to simultaneously study their habits, health, mental states, and values. In addition, they received Finland's existing "free" health care and education (nothing is free, but there are no out of pocket costs, if you don't count taxes which are pretty hefty). Would it be psychologically and physically toxic to be on the dole? We won't know from the Fins' social experiment because they shut it down after two years, at the end of 2018. Public opinion and cost burden were its ruin. The Fins were on the brink of giving us answers about what might happen to an unemployed yet supported workforce. But no longer. Perhaps other nations or enlightened social entrepreneurs will undertake such a societal investigation. Perhaps, the natural devolution of work itself may reveal answers to the loss of jobs that seems ahead.

Yet, for me, work is and has been since I was a boy "baked-in." I am uneasy, listless, if I am not working (and a lot in my case). As a psychiatrist, I am convinced that work, purposeful activities with personal and/or social meaning (whether paid or not), is the best antidepressant we have—if an individual can summon the energy and will to contribute their unique value to a family, community, or enterprise.

Work, in its many forms, transports us from the everyday ennui, from our aches and pains (though not manual labor). Time becomes timeless when we are mentally engaged. Self-preoccupations or quotidian externalities tend to fade into the background. Most all productive activities provide us with a sense of accomplishment, a job done, sometimes well done, evidence of our skill or service, not to mention money in many instances. More on this later, but back to the past, and with it a glimpse at today.

It was 1953 when I began my first job, unpaid but still laborious, as I described in the story anteceding these comments. I was eight years old and coming of age in America's 1950s.

The early '50s saw Harry S. Truman give way to Dwight Eisenhower (Ike) as the President, the latter a great war hero (the Supreme Commander of the Allied troops), a Republican, and a chain smoker. Richard Nixon was his vice president; it took him a while, two subsequent presidents, before he entered the White House, not distinguishing the executive office, as we know. Ike is credited with easing the cold war with the (then) Soviet Union. No small matter, since the Soviets had developed a hydrogen bomb, which became further impetus for the arms race, an international contest that would preoccupy our country for years to come. Absurdly, children (like myself) practiced air raids by hiding under our feeble, wooden desks. The Soviets crushed anti-government protests in East Germany in 1953.

The "Red Scare" about Communism escalated, with the FBI rounding up those considered to be Communists. In 1954, Senator Joseph McCarthy alarmed and disgraced this country by conducting a Congressional witch-hunt against suspected Communists, while all the time himself a hidden morphine addict (*The Addiction Solution*, Sederer, LI, Scribner, 2018). He held federal hearings against "known Communists," as well as outspoken social critics on his "black (or was it 'red?') list." In 1953, Ethel and Julius Rosenberg were executed in the electric chair as capital punishment after they had been convicted for conspiracy to commit espionage.

Queen Elizabeth II was crowned in Britain, upon the death of her father, King George, the fifth. She reigns to today. A mélange of great films and TV about this reticent and so very well-mannered monarch have capitalized on her persona and the character of the Brits during the decades of her rule.

The Korean War ended, though we still have its remnants in the demilitarized, dividing border between the South and the North, the 38th parallel line. Perhaps with tensions recently abating? We shall see. Cambodia ended 90 years of French colonial rule, further inspiring the drive to independence by many countries from their Colonial

European rulers. Albert Schweitzer received the Nobel Peace Prize.

In science, the polio vaccine was developed against a virus discovered near to 50 years earlier; Jonas Salk and his team of scientists cultivated the inactivated vaccine, which he gave to himself and his family to demonstrate its safety. James Watson and Francis Crick gave us the double-helix model of DNA, a wonder of a discovery, winning them the Nobel Prize (though not until early in the next decade). New York hung its first tricolor traffic lights, and cigarette smoking was reported as causing lung cancer (an initial shot across the bow, buried for years by Big Tobacco, as was the fate of many smokers). The United States tested the Hydrogen Bomb.

In popular culture, Ian Fleming published his first James Bond novel, and America saw its first Corvette. Playboy magazine had its first issue in 1953, with Marilyn Monroe on the cover and adorning the nude centerfold; it sold for 50 cents. Technology further blossomed with color now possible on new TVs (which cost a fortune, over $1,000 at the time) and radios going transistor. Sir Edmund Hillary, a New Zealander, and Tenzing Norgay, Nepalese, were the first to reach the summit of Everest. Men dressed up in cuff links, tie clips, and pleated pants. Women wore gowns, jumpers, print dresses, and nylon stockings; some even wore pants. More about fashion later on in this book. The great New York Yankees, my home team in the Bronx, won their fifth (!) World Series in a row.

Films that attracted attention included *Peter Pan (Disney), Some Like It Hot (Marilyn again), From Here to Eternity, Shane,* and *The Robe.* At the 25th Academy

Awards, Cecil B. DeMille won Best Picture for (not) *The Greatest Show on Earth*, Gary Cooper was best actor in *High Noon*, and Shirley Booth best actress in *Come Back, Little Sheba* (memorable title but not so for the film). Arthur Miller's *The Crucible* opened on Broadway.

In other words, the world was exploding about me as I humbly went about my latency years while unconsciously absorbing into my brain cells and psyche the power, the necessity, of work.

Barry Schwartz's small (yet large in scope) book *Why We Work* (Ted Books, Simon & Schuster, 2015) takes us into the non-material drivers of work. Work can challenge us, stretch our brains and creativity, and surprise and gratify the person who is making the effort. Work often, as well, provides us with a community, a social network, if not friends. Work allows a person to feel dignity, to be contributing to family and others, or advancing a worthy cause. Those people who are satisfied with their work describe it as purposeful, thereby generating meaning in their lives. And a lifetime of work well done, as Erik Erikson taught us, allows for our later years to be experienced as generative rather than darkened by despair.

Money is a necessary but often insufficient reward for working. Work that is repetitive and without felt social or familial value can be deadening. Those who feel a degree of passion for what they do are apt to be far more engaged and can even feel like work is not really work, in its literal sense. Incentives, therefore, that rely heavily on wages have their limits, despite some prevailing views of capitalism. It may be why so some employers complain they "just can't get good help." When work feels to be more of a "calling," it becomes not just a job.

I didn't become a doctor for the money. And certainly not a psychiatrist if I was looking to make a lot of money. I was intrigued by the mind and the brain, by the mysteries of human behavior and feelings, and the opportunity to get past thinking of myself by caring for others.

The future design and nature of work, or not working when robots claim a great deal of what has heretofore been human labor, will have to change if our societies are going to not be zombies, walking dead without direction or value. To find answers to the huge enigma of what will work become, a conceptual abyss facing this country and those not already living in dire poverty and hunger, may I suggest we look for guidance by asking what gives a person meaning, a sense of dignity, a purpose here on earth?

When my father, a prodigious worker and product of the Great Depression, finally sold his final business and went into retirement, he had enough money to live comfortably. But he lost his *raison d'être*. Plus, he was no golfer; he didn't even drink. He became depressed, the kind of unhappiness that is not very responsive to anti-depressants. There was no channel for his energy, no demands upon his still active brain, no community, and no way for him to be the competitive man he was. He finally died of lung cancer, having smoked heavily until well into his 40s, but his heart had already gone dead. He went without raging against the night.

I am among the fortunate who was bred to work at an early age, whose race and social circumstances and the growing prosperity and (for some) meritocracy of the 1950s in America, permitted me the opportunity to make a living, to have a calling, to be part of a community. To love and respect, and to feel deeply grateful (most every day, when I have my head about me) for my time on earth.

May you love your work, hold yourself high with your own form of earned self-esteem, and have a life of contribution. That will be wealth of the finest sort, a blessing bestowed upon you.

*****

Chapter 2
The Evening Paper

At about 7:30 pm or so, after a weekday dinner was over, my father used to leave the house, get in his big boat of a new Oldsmobile, 4 doors with a muted two-tone exterior, and return a half-hour later. I never knew where he went. Then one day, maybe when I was about nine, he said "come with me," which I conspiratorially did. We drove nearby to an outdoor newsstand at the bottom of a dark, steep stairwell to the elevated subway in the northeast Bronx, near Pelham Parkway. He gave me a coin and told me to buy the evening edition of the Times or Herald Tribune, I can't remember which. But I felt swell. I had been charged with some crucial, invaluable task.

My dad rapidly extracted the paper from my grip and began to page through the financial section, where the day's stock market results were reported. Clearly, this was before a person could examine the financial "pages," at any moment, on their smartphone or laptop. For my father, the evening paper was a daily ritual, like praying is for some people. He glanced at a few select stock closing quotes, muttered a word or two aloud about their respective results, saving a more detailed review until he got home. The company names he uttered meant nothing to me, even far less than their closing exchange numbers. But I was privy to his thinking, his scheming, and to any financial gains that pleased him or losses he suffered that day, which I could understand mattered in one (good) direction, or another (not so good). He liked playing the stock market.

My father was a trader, as they have been called then and now. He was a gambler too (if that is any different?). He also played cards, especially gin rummy, in a game that rotated monthly to our living room at 3100 Eastchester Road. We moved there when I was five, fleeing what came to be called "Fort Apache," the dangerous neighborhoods of the South Bronx. Our home was an attached, red brick, row house, which sat at the end of the block, so we had only one next-door neighbor as well as a side lawn, so to speak. Lots of scraggly hedges too, which were my job to trim.

My grandparents (on my mother's side) lived in the small, one-bedroom, one-bathroom apartment on the ground floor. My parents, younger sister, Marge, and I on the upper two, narrow floors, in three small bedrooms. There was even a driveway, a one-car garage that barely accommodated a '50s car, and a front porch. We had come up in life.

My dad loved, as well, to play the horses – the flats and the trotters. Sometimes I got to go on the weekend or during the summer, to Aqueduct or Belmont Raceway, with their gorgeous steeds with jockeys atop of them, or to Yonkers Raceway to bet on the horse-drawn, racing carriages. It was exhilarating to see those massive animals at full stride, to have bet two dollars on one to win or draw (not place, which is third, and offered little return because it was less risky).

And then to feel the rush of victory or pain of defeat once the horses crossed to finish line. I mostly would glumly toss the losing pari-mutuel to the ground and turn to my selections for the next race. To my amazement, I occasionally would win and take my precious betting ticket to the windows to be paid off. That's when I could feel the adrenaline, like I was diving off a cliff.

My father, Ruby—as he was called—traded adventurously in the stock exchange. Over time, he lost a lot of the family money, but he made a good deal of it back before he died, riding the 1990s market boom. Thank god he was on the winning side when he passed since my mother then could be financially secure. After his death, I looked at his stock portfolio on behalf of my mother: he held shares in 120 different companies, on various exchanges. It was like he had been working for an over-the-top, cocaine-fueled brokerage company (one you would not want to trust with your savings). But he didn't need amphetamines to drive him, nor the nearby shouts of other traders to egg him on. It seemed impossible to me, after assembling a list of his holdings, to imagine monitoring, no less managing, them, even if I didn't try to replicate his daily market transactions. I marveled at my father's tolerance for risk, incessant focus, and acumen. He did have the gaming thing bad, that was apparent; it didn't take a psychiatrist (which I had been for some time by then) to see. The first thing I did was to simplify the portfolio, selling and consolidating into far fewer stocks, and some bonds. I am sure I reduced its future value, but the risk was too great for me to bear. I was always a chicken when it came to money.

But I did catch the gambling itch, from the time I started at Bronx Science. I would play seven-card stud poker with fellow high school students, in the Bronx or Northern Manhattan. at one of their homes—never mine since that would, ironically, not be permitted by my father. I won more than I lost. I don't recall deliberately counting cards but I kept my eye on the open ones, trying to calculate my odds, and had a sense of when another player was bluffing or not. Everyone has "tells," if you watch close enough.

I also would skip school—maybe once a month during horse racing season—and go with a fellow Science student-gambler to Belmont or Aqueduct (which were possible to get to by train, unlike Yonkers Raceway). I had a false ID but no one at the gate seemed to care. I would study the racing form, a horse's past performance against the timing of the competition, at what track, distances, and conditions (dry, muddy, fast, or slow), and the like, and come to my considered decision. I ran to the betting windows, stood in line waiting my turn, ahead of track time and the closing bell, burying my head in my chin trying not to be discovered to be the underage truant I was. The rush was fantastic. But, as previously noted, I usually lost on my $2 bets.

Sometimes, when not absconding to the track, I would read the racing form in homeroom, at school, and later go to a convenience store near Science where a bookie would take a bet. This clearly was not normal, but what was normal, what we saw on the TV sitcoms of the 1950s? My dad or mom didn't know what mischief I was up to, I think. Or maybe they did? Families have—and keep—their secrets. They quietly condone some behaviors and rail against others. Gambling was intrinsic to my father's life. Why not mine as well?

I kept up the poker playing into medical school because it provided a net gain in my meager economic standing. But then I stopped, never to have the itch again—for any form of gaming. Casinos bored me. The race track became more of a fantastic sporting event than a place to gamble. But not so for my father, who gambled to his last days.

For me, however, it was like a monkey had been taken off my back: I had enough of gambling like a '60s stoner gets over smoking pot or a '70s young professional gets over snorting cocaine. For some, these compulsive activities abate. Public health doctors like me ponder why that happens, but we don't know for sure. Biology, psychology, social circumstance interplay in creating risky behaviors, and in mitigating them. We can speculate, but not truly know.

But I do understand when and how an addiction can begin.

*****

2A: Fathers, Sons, and Gambling Too

Being a son is like being a guest in your father's home, to paraphrase Evelyn Waugh. A son has no right to expect much, and no quarter in which to file his grievances. He does not get to make the rules. A son has been given temporary quarters, and traditionally was expected to contribute to the household. Father and son usually each strive in opposing ways, the father to keep the family safe and together, the son to leave it.

Yet, as a son and a psychiatrist for a long time now (not to mention being a father myself), I see how enormous are the forces pulling father and son together—and forcing them apart. Perhaps the deepest of the former are what are known as "identification." Without trying and unbeknownst to the son, he is absorbing his father into his psyche, into his nature: thinking like him, acting like him (literally and figuratively), treating others as did his father. Sometimes, the tensions get too high, as the son's need to be separate, be different, evokes animus on both sides of the familial dynamic. Freud made a big deal about the Oedipus triangle, the son competing for his father's wife, otherwise known as his mother. I am not big on that legendary theory and don't think there is any science to prove it. I also thought my mother's (Harriet), younger, rather histrionic sister, Muriel, was the most beautiful woman in the world; it was she, not my mother, I coveted. Plus, I had other women, my grandmothers, to dote on me, to shower me with affection.

I don't recall my father's father. He had died when I was very young. He had been an immigrant from Eastern Europe, and I assume modeled the unceasing and prodigious work that so clearly represented who my dad was. Which is to say that I grew up in the home of a man, the father of the family, who never stopped working and striving, who aimed to be accepted by those whom he admired—usually prosperous businessmen.

My father had addictions to gambling and cigarettes. It was tobacco, which he had quit in his forties, that killed him, from recurrent, adenomas cell cancer of the lungs.

Gambling is but one of a number of human foibles considered addictions; serious problems in which a person, man or woman, engages in compulsive behaviors despite their major adverse consequences, like to health, work, relationships, and financial stability.

Not that long ago, the American Psychiatric Association designated gambling an addiction, adding it to drinking, smoking, and drugs. All of them were compulsive, which meant they were very hard to resist. What was new, different, about gambling was that it was a behavioral addiction, not to an ingested or inhaled substance. Yet gambling is powerfully doing something to change the brain; when done repetitively, over time, it has its price. We now know it fires the same neural brain regions as do cocaine, opioids, and other drugs—the pleasure centers, in the brain, where it releases a burst of dopamine.

An addiction does not signal that a person is bad, or weak. Though that has been a stubborn societal conviction because those in the throes of an addiction frequently do bad things, like steal, lie, and betray. They do so to support their habit or stave off the misery of withdrawal. Often, a person uses more than one substance: for example, alcohol and tranquilizers, opioid pain pills and cannabis (about 10% of frequent users of pot also develop a physical and emotional dependence on this drug). Video games are near to achieving the status of a behavioral addiction; though, of course, only when their activity begins to take over a person's life. Video gambling is highly addictive, perhaps related to the rapidity of its stimulation on brain reward (dopamine) centers. Sexual addiction, increasingly in the news, seems to me to be mostly about power, narcissism, and deep insecurity, not quite like substances and gambling.

We have learned a lot more about addiction in recent years. We know the locations of human cerebral reward centers, specifically the nucleus accumbens and ventral tegmental area. These are the sites where a dopamine burst fires and generates the wonderful feeling we call pleasure. The accelerator pedal, if you will, that adds emotive gas to our lives and drives repetitive action. A brain circuit is ignited, so to speak, by these neural complexes and their release of dopamine, reaching our motivational center, the orbitofrontal cortex. That's where we involuntarily, automatically, have the experience of, "I liked that," and, "I want more of that."

Our memories (of pleasure as well as danger or pain) are encoded, over time, in the amygdala and hippocampus. They take the form, principally, of cues that enable us to remember the sources of pleasure and pain, like sights, sounds, smells, tastes, and the like. These cues become critical "triggers" that induce, in addiction, a craving for more of that source(s) of comfort, pleasure, or relief of pain. Triggers are the main drivers of relapse, potentially forever, even after an extended period of abstinence has been achieved. Think of people you know who were in recovery for years, then something changed in their lives; these encoded triggers were re-ignited and, literally overnight, they were again heavily using.

The force of our brain's reward circuit can be mighty. After all, it also serves our needs for hunger and sex, instincts that are hard to not satisfy if we are to survive and procreate. Dr. Nora Volkow, director of the National

Institute on Drug Abuse, has said that addiction "pirates the brain," namely takes hostage a person's everyday life and values by robbing us of our everyday sources of pleasure. That's what makes the need (the craving) for the drug (or related, reward-inducing activity) paramount, giving supremacy to the addiction over just about every other aspect of a person's life.

Addictions are hard to beat. They seize us in two ways: first, as sources of pleasure and second, as sources of craving (their withdrawal states) when the reward begins to wear off. Those, for example, addicted to alcohol and a variety of other psychoactive (mind-altering) substances, including opioids, amphetamines, and benzodiazepams, experience withdrawal when the circuitry of pleasure is diminished in its activity. This state of misery happens when brain firing and blood levels of the substance decline: Our cerebral cells and pathways, as well as parts of our body like the gut, had grown accustomed to the drug or compulsive behavior. The source of pleasure is waning, and we feel what can amount to an intense drive to restore our feelings to the levels of gratification of the "high"—or, after longer-term use, to reduce the awful symptoms of withdrawal, like severe anxiety, sweating, vomiting, tremor, diarrhea, and the like. Withdrawal is always at bay after dependence sets in: Our body comes to crave the substance or behavior that was the source of reward, or to counter its absence. Regaining even a measure of that gratification or calming withdrawal pain comes to dominate the thinking and behaviors of an addicted person.

Moreover, typically accompanying longer-term use and dependence is what is termed "tolerance." This physiological state results in a need for higher doses of the substance (or reward evoking stimulus) to achieve the same experience of pleasure or relief of withdrawal pain. What we see, for example, is a person consuming even higher amounts of alcohol or doses of a drug or given to higher stakes and more frequent gambling.

My father had developed a compulsive, addictive relationship to the stock market. He had an abundant portfolio, typical of an investment fund (not an individual), comprised of stocks as well as "options" to buy and sell high or short, on several exchanges. His daily buying and selling of equities was characteristic of the condition of addiction, which grew in him over the years. His addictions extended to playing the horses and cards. He never went to GA (Gamblers Anonymous); I don't know if it existed back then. Yet his gambling never put in peril our housing, food for dinner, or his businesses. Thinking back on his life, that clearly was what he loved to do. Turns out, over his lifetime, he became pretty good at it, better at the stock market and cards than the track, from what I surmised after he was gone.

I was drawn to what he did, and who he was. Maybe it was an innate, biological disposition, or the psychological phenomenon of identification mentioned earlier. Maybe we both needed to transport ourselves from the everyday and mundane, from the grind of quotidian existence. Likely all of those. Another factor in addiction, as well, is what was (is) available, readily accessible to us as individuals in our respective generations, whether legally and otherwise. Access is a proven element, public health knowledge tells us, about what gets used and onto what a person becomes hooked. I loved cards, horses, and, with my father's help, bought some cheap stock options when I was a teenager (probably from my Bar Mitzvah money). Like a number of Philip Roth's prototypical characters, I too was obsessed with sex. Later, in college, I enjoyed my share of alcohol and marijuana, but only on weekends (!).

In public health, we think about addictions not just in chemical terms, or brain circuitry gone haywire, but related to the conditions of a person's life. These are considered developmental *risk and protective* factors.

Risk factors for addiction include a parent or other close relative dependent on alcohol or drugs (or gambling); an active mental illness in the home, such as depression or psychosis; as well as, commonly, childhood trauma, from neglect or abuse. Adult trauma from war, forced emigration, or a natural disaster, such as a hurricane, fire, or flood, are also risk factors for addiction (and other conditions). We see those impacted by disaster using more of or abusing tobacco, alcohol, and drugs.

Protective factors that help prevent or limit the gravity of an addiction include the good fortune to have had supportive, engaged families and households, free of violence and addiction. Faith in a higher power, whether in a formal religion or not (as in spirituality), is a strong protective factor and a vital tool in recovery for those who develop an addiction and seek to regain their footing in life. Education and employment opportunities are protective as well.

I had a lot of protective factors, and not that many that put me at risk. My scale was leaning in the right direction.

My father, the only son of his mother's only marriage to a widowed man with children of his own, held a special place in his mother's life. But the home was burdened by the poverty, hunger, and persistent hopelessness of the Great Depression. They lived in a tenement, among a gaggle of fellow immigrants from Italy, Ireland, and Eastern Europe. There was no one on their side. No education to be had for his parents, and only high school for my father. Their neighborhood was safe if a bit Anti-Semitic. Opportunity was what they made from their limited prospects and, I imagine, unlimited grit. I doubt his parents gambled—no money for that, and it was a rare Jew who drank, other than on Holy Days, weddings, Bar Mitzvahs, and when sitting *Shiva* (the mourning rite, for as long as a week after a death).

My family's story (on both sides, focused here on my father) makes me proud of America, how something could be made from virtually nothing (material), by a whole lot of hard work and perseverance. Ours is a country built by immigrants. There was xenophobia in the '50s (and the Red Scare), but not the lawless and cruel governmental type that has emerged in recent years in this country, and other nations around the globe. Immigrants arrived, back then, seeking safety, jobs and, in time, to be able to build families, aiming to give their children more than they had. Immigrants still want the same today, but borders are tight, and entry often gained surreptitiously, especially along our southern frontier.

We are amidst an epidemic of addiction, most prominently to opioids. Yet, it is still tobacco and alcohol that are the principal, preventable killers. I proffer a public health approach to mitigating the addiction epidemic, public health being the specialty I have learned much about over the past two decades. We have seen incredible successes, in the US and abroad, that beat back infectious diseases like polio and smallpox; how sanitation averted countless water-borne diseases; how tobacco and driving deaths have been substantially reduced; how after the kind of public groundswell we could use today for opioid dependence, we ended the HIV/AIDs epidemic.

A public health approach to a disorder (or deadly behaviors) is built on well-known foundations: prevention, screening (like we now have for high blood pressure, diabetes, high lipid levels, and cancers of various types), which permits early detection and treatment, almost always more successful than when the condition grows deeper roots over time, and the affordable, accessible delivery of proven treatments. When we knit these elements together, we stand a very good chance of success.

And more than ever, we have come to appreciate the power of our respective social circumstances, of the "social determinants of health and illness." These, indeed, are the most difficult to change, since we enter the realms of poverty, domestic violence, safety in neighborhoods, food insecurity, safe and reliable housing, and equitable and quality education, from pre-school on. *Only 10%* of our health is a product of the healthcare we receive; the balance is due to these (and related) social determinants of health. Paula Lantz, a British economist, remarked (and I paraphrase) that Americans tend to confound health with healthcare. The magnitude of these social problems notwithstanding, we can break them down into smaller, incremental and feasible ways to make a difference.

The sooner we start, the better. I was fortunate. So many others are not. Their suffering and huge economic costs are a baleful measure of the humanity of a country, our country, and a yardstick against which to judge the efforts we endeavor to make.

*****

Chapter 3
Lloyd's Supermarket

When I was young, less than five, my family lived in the South Bronx, on Fox Street, in a walk-up tenement. My father was running a corner grocery store, diagonally across from our building, which he had inherited from his parents after working there for many years.

But after their death and then some, he sold it. He bought a small supermarket on Dyckman Street, in Washington Heights, which is at the top, left part of Manhattan when you look at a map of the city, like a view from a satellite brought to you by Google. Unbeknownst to me, after he did some renovations before re-opening it, he put up a sign running along the top of the store's long, glass windows, which themselves displayed a ménage of non-perishable products as well as posters exclaiming the bargains to be had. The sign above the store announced its name: *Lloyd's Supermarket*.

Far as I know, there is only one Lloyd in our family. My father, as well, was not much of an Anglophile, nor did he have money invested in Lloyd's of London, the famed insurance firm. This name of the supermarket had to be a reference to me. Given how he hardly said a word to me, this maybe was some big statement on his part, though more likely he did it for my mother, a very sweet woman, who worked there too just as she did in the grocery store. Maybe he was declaring that I would be working there soon enough, which actually didn't happen because he sold it by the time I was eight, which would have been just old enough to have enslaved me there on weekends and extracted some work out of the likes of me.

On Saturdays, which were the busiest days, we all piled into the family car, a post-war big 1950s Oldsmobile (he liked those) and drove south from the Bronx where we lived to the supermarket. We parked nearby (not a furious competition like it would be today), piled out, and marched to the store's door, which he unlocked for the long day ahead. It was our job, my sister Marge and me, to stay out of the way. She was, still is, three years younger than me, and was much more able to follow that instruction than I.

The first to arrive, after us, was the greengrocer. An Italian guy, big smile, who really knew his fruits and vegetables. He had the most to do, besides my parents. He needed to fill up the wooden stands to receive the fresh produce, to make those tomatoes shine and the lettuce not look like it spent the night in the alley. Other employees trundled in. Just a few, I mean this was not *Whole Foods*. My mother worked one of the three cash registers. The other two were generally dormant like they were waiting for business to sprout like spring flowers. My father did about everything, not to mention wandering about, intent on having the employees do their job, as the captain of the *Lloyd's Supermarket* enterprise, and to keep stealing to a minimum.

By early afternoon, I (and even my sister) had become a nuisance. We were often in the way, wasting needed time to mind us when they needed to be running the store. I can't recall how often, but pretty often, I was given some money and told to take my sister (and me) to the movies, the "matinee" if you will, at a theatre a couple of blocks away. It was on the same side of the street, as I recall, so I was less apt to kill the both of us crossing the very wide avenue that Dyckman Street was, even though it was not called an avenue. I loved the movies, still do, but not having to take my younger sister. She knew I was not happy to have her along, so she tended to trail me by a foot or two to elude my grumpiness.

There were newsreels, cartoons (!), and a movie, sometimes two, with a plot that typically portrayed how life in America was just peachy. This was the early '50s, mind you. I don't recall receiving any coins to buy popcorn. It was not sold in the supermarket back then, not even potato chips.

Once the show was over, the movie theatre lights would go on and it was time to leave. Now late in the afternoon, I would head us back to *Lloyd's Supermarket*. By that time of day, business was brisk, pretty intense—not quite like *Fairway* or *Wholefoods* in New York City, but still busy—particularly before dinnertime on Saturday. We were, thus, relegated to the "office," if that is what you could call the partitioned cubicle in the back, until the customers subsided. Only then would we again be allowed to free range, like the types of chickens served in premiere restaurants nowadays. As the day began to end, the greengrocer undid all his careful work. Many of the other employees left. The cash registers were emptied and tallied. My father locked the doors, reversing the morning ritual, and we went home. I have no idea what time that was, but I thought it was at least midnight. The store was closed on Sundays. The good old days.

One of my many regrets is that I never asked my dad (or my mother who might have offered more of an explanation) why he named the store *Lloyd's Supermarket*. His had to be the ruling decision, as were just about all the final decisions in the household, though my mother always had a say, with her clear voice and opinions. As I said, she must have had something to do with naming the store for their firstborn son. My dad was a complicated, reticent man, a driven and formidable worker, a step-son when his mother remarried and had more kids to mind, and a product of immigrant roots amplified by the Great Depression.

The supermarket prospered after a few years of my family's hard work and good business sense. By then, more than one cash-register was frequently open. Goods frequently were delivered by the front since there was no rear loading dock. A success story. But my father became restless again. He decided to sell the business and fetched a good price from what I deduce. I say this because we drove to Florida for a very long vacation, open-ended. Getting there was an endless ride; one reason seemed to be that my sister got car sick a lot. So we had to stop, again and again as I recall, to keep the back seat free of her stomach contents.

We returned from Florida to New York City after a while. I later overheard that was because my father didn't find a business he wanted to buy there. He didn't seem to work for ages, though it was probably less than a year; he was around the house a lot. When he went out during the day, it was to spend time at a nearby stock brokerage office, not as an employee but to read the ticker tapes and buy and sell stocks; he was what we call today a "trader." He managed to stay financially whole, maybe made some money during that interlude, because he then moved onto his next business, the one I complain about in Chapter 1.

I moved back to NYC in 2002, after living for 36 years as an NYC refugee in disparate cities and towns in America's east. I decided, one Saturday, to drive to Dyckman Street, from Lower Manhattan where I was living. I knew without directions exactly where the store would be. There it was, now a type of dollar store, with posters shouting, "everything reduced to go." There was no sign saying *Lloyd's Supermarket*, except in my head.

*****

3A: Family Businesses

The "business" was the nexus of our family. Both my parents worked in the business(es) as they progressed from grocery and stationery stores to a supermarket and an office supply company. Weekends often were times to be at the business. Dinner conversation was dominated by the business. The family enterprise was the lens that refracted so much of the light that entered our home.

My sister Marge (and her husband) established, first located in SoHo (the New York term referring to the area south of Houston Street), a very successful archival art supply family business. That was after my father abruptly sold the office supply company to a bigger fish, and moved to Florida, thereby soon ending my brother-in-law's job. Two of the three kids (adults now) that my sister and brother-in-law have, are working in and now running their company (as they gently succeed their parents). The DNA of a family business has now been replicated into the third generation of my Eastern Europe forebears.

McKinsey Consulting reported, in 2010, that less than 30% of family businesses survive into the third generation of ownership. McKinsey was particularly interested in iconic or mammoth family enterprises, those families that sit atop corporations like the New York Times or Walmart. But as intriguing as those may be, they do not constitute the majority we see in our country. Instead, these are the local grocery (or bodega), clothing, tailoring and dry-cleaning stores, restaurants and bars, bakeries and street vendors, the family farm, car dealers, repair shops of all stripes, and even those clans that grow (or synthesize) and distribute drugs. And so on. These are fundamental building blocks and paths to success in America, more so than working for others in companies, institutions, and corporations (financial services excepted). Later on, the professions and the arts may prevail in a family, but that is very unusual at the beginning of the immigrant family's journey.

What makes for a successful family business? Both economically and interpersonally? Success is by no means a given in these varied forms of commerce. I have escaped the world of family business by becoming a doctor, and even my father was OK with that (maybe because it was my Jewish mother's dream her son become a doctor). But I am no stranger to the trials a family undergoes pursuing and managing ownership of whatever may be their métier.

Perhaps most important to success is an enduring bond among family members. The powerful, if unspoken, commitment to each other—and to not fail. The trust that must be nurtured and sustained principally, I think, by putting family first and foremost. These are the ingredients of the secret sauce of a family in general, and fundamental to managing a business together. Of course, the vagaries of the marketplace will have their way, say if you went down because you were still trying to sell household coal or horseshoes or petticoats.

Like in all relationships, the ability to talk openly with one another is a prize to seek. Sometimes that calls for "family meetings," to do the hard work of communicating ideas and solving problems. But those are infrequent, at most, and need to be amplified by the quotidian exchanges with one another other, which are endless. Words are the material from which bridges are built between us; the means by which we can daily touch one another's minds and hearts, create a milieu of being in it all together, tackle endless problems, small and large, and deliver the salve needed to heal the wounds of family friction.

What can readily spoil a family's business are conflicts over money and authority: these may be like the X and Y axes of a graph, where unrest is linearly associated with growth on either or both measures. For family-owned larger or corporate enterprises, nepotism is poisonous, particularly when it results in poor financial and human relations performance. Families need to be mindful of the undercurrents of conflict among their members, and the in-laws. The drivers of unrest are legion but at the top are power battles and the process of succession in ownership and authority (or actual governance), particularly among the nuclear family and their spouses or partners. The family dynamics we might experience are usually not as dramatic as the TV programs *Dynasty* and *The Sopranos*. But they can create an operetta of their own.

The transition of ownership and stewardship from one generation to another is often tricky. After all, one generation has devoted their life to get where they are in business today and the next generation can't help but feel uncertain about the financial viability of what lies ahead. Technology moves fast and adds fuel to the contests between the old and the new.

What corporations and institutions call "governance"— who has authority over what, when, and how—is also a feature of smaller enterprises. And it is a big deal, no matter what the annual operating budget may be. Learning how to be clear, informed, consistent, and respectful goes a long way. Sometimes governance is bedeviled by the tension inherent between parents and their children, or individuals and their spouses. Culture intrudes here as well, since being an elder, even being a man, still holds valence in many an ethnic group.

I know a number of psychologists and social workers who have specialized in family businesses—not in running one but offering a forum for when family matters seem to have gone aground.

When I was in Cambridge, MA, in the 1980s, I trained in family therapy. Not so much for helping families navigate working together but for helping families succeed when faced, for example, with physical and mental illnesses, with addiction, aging, financial strains, parenting, divorce, and whatever else may have beset them. The training has helped me in my work as a clinician and an administrator. It took much longer for me to follow my own counsel at home. This is one time that aging, more like maturing and learning from my mistakes, I suppose, can help.

All that said, my hat is off to my parents and my sister's family as they daily manage(d) both life and business together, now over scores of decades, with their countless dilemmas and moments of interaction.

I sometimes ask, what has been my "*Lloyd's Supermarket*?" What have been the work settings where my leadership and drive, my attention to what works and who works there, and to the measures of success (in medicine, those are quality and financial sustainability)? I hope I have attended to these matters throughout my many jobs, from running an inpatient psychiatric unit, an outpatient clinic or as medical director of a psychiatric hospital, or producing treatment guidelines and quality measure for the field of psychiatry, and to my work in both municipal and state government. But it was my time, 11 years in all, at McLean Hospital, a Harvard-teaching psychiatric hospital in Belmont, Massachusetts (right outside of Cambridge and across the Charles River from Boston), that was then my biggest professional leap and a totally hands-on position. That might best exemplify my immersion in what could be seen as my *Lloyd's Supermarket*.

I was recruited there by my great friend and psychiatric colleague Steven Mirin, MD. He had returned to work there the year before to run the clinical and research services. But abruptly, the head of the hospital, called the Psychiatrist-in-Chief, a beloved Texan named Dr. Sherv Frazier, stepped down after questions about plagiarism in his medical writings. As much as this was a misdemeanor at best, given the material identified, the outcome was as if felonious. He vanished from the professional scene after the briefest time spent explaining to Steve how to run the hospital.

Which was a lot to learn. McLean was then, still is, iconic: arguably one of the finest private, not-for-profit, academic, psychiatric hospitals in the world. It was established in 1819, so my arrival there was 170 years after its inception. McLean had the reputation of caring for the rich, celebrities, faculty, and students from Harvard, MIT and the abundance of universities in the Boston area. There was a joke that it was harder to get into McLean (as a patient!) than it was to gain admission to Harvard College. The 20 years before my taking a job there had been successful for the institution. Its 325 inpatient beds nearly were always full, as were the many private pay cottages on the 246-acre Olmstead-designed campus, which had the largest collection of decorative trees in Massachusetts, after the Arnold Arboretum. McLean had, as well, robust programs in clinical and basic science research underway, adding to its luster, reputationally and economically.

But a tsunami was on the horizon. The McLean Board of Trustees saw it coming, thanks to Mirin and some others. In 1989, Managed Care, the dark enemy of medical services, had entered the state. It would have the power to set hospital prices (daily inpatient rates and other charges), slash lengths of stay (LOS, how many days a patient remained in the hospital), and deny admission to many in need, especially at first to those with substance use disorders. Its sharpest sword was to decide which hospitals patients could use, their "approved" network of facilities, which was and continues to be a source of bitter contention among insured people, their families, and their doctors.

McLean would clearly be in their cross-hairs: its LOS at the time was 63 days, while MGH Psychiatry (where I had been only seven years earlier) was 14 days; the per diem rate (price) at McLean was near to 50% higher than other, local hospitals, academic and community; admission was burdensome and selective; the psychiatric staff principally operated on a fee-for-service model, where patient coverage was at the mercy of the wishes of the private doctors (with free offices on the grounds, which proved to run counter to federal regulation)—whose additional charges were typically not covered by the state's managed care plans. You see the picture—though few of the professional and administrative staff did at the time. Present-day hindsight was needed and generally was not welcomed.

Mirin needed a medical director for him to attend to the massive responsibilities he had suddenly inherited. The Medical Director was responsible for the clinical services, which had to be overhauled: LOS had to be progressively reduced, expenses cut, and, for the first time, care made accessible to patients on government entitlement programs, especially Medicaid (the state-federal program that covered the indigent). McLean had to institute a staff model of care, in which the doctors worked for the hospital, thereby assuring their attention to all patients. Diversity had to be introduced to the clinical programming (it had solely relied on inpatient care and revenue), which meant opening outpatient clinics, day programs, half-way houses—even delivering services off the campus, in the community.

Someone had to be fool enough to wrestle with these bears. Steve asked me to join him, and a few other missionaries to make it happen, for me to become McLean's Medical Director. My hire happened over tuna fish sandwiches in his corner office in McLean's grand "Admin" Building, on a glass table between the couches, which he sprayed with Windex when we were done. It was not the first time I leaped off a cliff, but it was then the highest peak I had encountered.

McLean was not a supermarket or an archival art supply company. It was not a family business unless you considered that to be its multigenerational, Boston Brahman Board. But for those of us selected to run the place at that time, the proverbial buck stopped with us, which seems no different from a family business in the mantle of responsibility we wore.

I was there early every day and always stayed late. Weekends were not time off. I got to know the nurses and doctors (MDs and PhDs), the aides, the social workers, the clerical staff spread over several dozen sites, the grounds and maintenance crews, the kitchen staff, and the Board, any and everyone who could bear spending any time with me. Some of the best managerial moments were our executive team meetings, regularly held on a Saturday, all day long, nourished by the bagels and lox that Mirin brought in, and our collective mission and spirit.

We were out to save a hospital, a feature of the Boston and national medical scene, a place for patients and families to seek and get good care. While my boss, Steve Mirin, did not feel like my father, he felt like my older brother; he has remained a close friend for 30 years. He even hired me again, when I left McLean, to head clinical services at the American Psychiatric Association, where he had gone when he left McLean when his mission there was accomplished.

To make a pretty long story short (covered back then in the Boston Globe's Sunday magazine, with a photo of Mirin and Sederer walking the grounds), the first five years were an uproar. Many there first thought us "crazy" to disrupt what had been more than two decades of stellar hospital performance. Do you know the curse, "May you have 20 years of success?" Later, many there reproached or just hated us.

The hospital hemorrhaged money for several years; there were two different efforts to buy us or close us down. The pace of change was furious, evoking calls to slow down, not move so fast. I made it a point to almost immediately install a host of clinical quality indicators (published then in a public and staff newsletter we called *McLean Reports*) so when those accustomed to the status quo claimed the "new administration" was destroying McLean, I would be able to show the evidence we were not. We published an extensive list of clinical measures, including outcomes and patient experience—for which we used valid and reliable instruments that we had developed solely for those two measures, called the BASIS-32 and The PoC (Perception of Care); we later licensed it to other hospitals.

We saved McLean. After near to ten years, its clinical profile looked radically different: LOS dropped to 14 days on average, and per diem costs were reduced by 40%; a staff model of care with near to 200 clinicians prospered; research grew; donor support increased; a section of the property was sold for high-end, housing development. But the operating inpatient beds were about half of where they were when we began. By the mid-90s, we were out of the red, and the hospital has remained so still today. I am told that the marginal losses now from inpatient care have been absorbed by the earnings from the portfolio of new services we generated during those turbulent years. We were the "generation" charged with saving a historical, storied hospital, and to leave it in good shape for the generation to come. It was a privilege bestowed upon our management group, and like any sizable privilege, conferred a sizable bundle of responsibilities.

That's my "family business" story, even if McLean was (is) no family business. I tried not to talk about it at the dinner table, but couldn't help myself.

*****

Chapter 4
The Accordion

My best guess is that I was about nine when my father drove us in his tank of an early '50s Oldsmobile, four doors with big white-wall tires, to mid-town Manhattan, to the music district on the west side. My mother must have put him up to doing this child development task, his fatherly duty. He hardly said a word in the car, usually never did to me, just smoked some unfiltered Camels and coughed a lot, a harbinger of the lung cancer that would kill him four decades later. I was by his side, holding his hand when began the Cheyne-Stokes, labored breathing that signals the very end of life. I watched as he then quietly ceased to be.

Back to the accordion story. We parked near one of those stores with a million gleaming guitars and drum sets in their glass windows, where people who knew how to play music went and knew what they were doing. We pushed through its heavy glass door and stared at the ocean of instruments. I was about to get my first musical instrument. I wanted an accordion.

Maybe it was from watching Lawrence Welk on TV, where Myron Floren, the lead accordionist, often stood before and sometimes led the big band. Or because

Lawrence himself would occasionally be even more of a show-off by playing one himself. The accordion somehow was what I had decided to play. Maybe also because it was a one-man band, more so than a piano or a guitar. I didn't know much about music, or have much exposure to it, except for the Sinatra, Garland and Welk I heard at home. That was about it, and the only Polish or German polkas and marches playing in my Jewish home were delivered by Welk and his entourage.

We left the shop, not with a child-sized accordion, but a full-sized one—brand new. When I sat with it in my lap in the front seat of the car, I was not visible from nor could I see through the windshield. I had long fingers (no Trump comparison intended) and could handle (no pun intended) the right-hand keyboard. My left hand was supposed to navigate a landscape of small, black buttons that could not really be seen, like spelunking with your headlamp broken. I think the price must have been right, or it had aged on the shelf, since my businessman of a father decided to buy it, and we soon were on the way home with my oversized accordion. It came in a big, wooden (or compressed-board) case, a sky-blue valise that today would never meet airplane carry-on limits or fit into the luggage rack space, even in first class. It was too heavy for me to pick up or carry more than a few feet, as I recall. So, we also bought small wheels that could be strapped to the bottom of the case, at the back, and then be tugged along city streets by the skinny kid I was.

I also bought sheet music that day and over time in the Bronx, lots of show tunes, marches, and waltzes, the stuff created for an accordion, which is like an entire compressed orchestra powered by a rectangular bellows. I soon had a teacher at a low-rent music studio near our house; once in a while, he came to our home, probably because it was more convenient for him at that moment, not to lavish attention, and certainly not earned by my caliber of play. He may have made those home visits because of my family's pleas to spend less time ferrying me about. I recall practicing conscientiously; I don't think I am lying about that. I say that with some confidence because my sister, Marge, didn't faithfully practice the upright piano in the living room, and was regularly judged in comparison to her more responsible, older brother.

The accordion is a noisy thing. It doesn't have a mute, not even like drums today. Its play was amplified, not by electricity or speakers, but by a bellows that could fan Hades. I was sort of blissed out by the sound, which helped me escape from endless preoccupation with myself, a popular youthful proclivity. I tried to sing along voicing some of the great Broadway lyrics but was so off-key, even I knew I was ruining the show, such as it was.

I guess I wasn't that bad because, for a couple of years, I played in the elementary school orchestra at P.S. 121—of course, the only accordion in the ensemble. But not quite like Myron Floren, who by the way sounds like he has a Jewish name, but I bet it is German. Too many anti-Semites back then. I actually had a bit of a life in elementary school, not to be sustained thereafter. I was in a number of school plays, had the lead once as Father Knickerbocker of New York; the plot—if there was one—escapes me. But I have a picture at home to prove it (my wife can provide collaborative information). I talked with girls, at least those who didn't ignore me. I was part of the human race, it seems, until the seventh grade, at which time I became a bit of a social pariah, not to be found as a member of my youthful community—for the familiar reasons of that age, in general, and to my particular asocial demeanor.

In 2003—a year after I returned to live and work in New York City, having been in self-imposed exile for 36 years—I was invited to be a *"Principal For A Day"* (a non-profit charity that paired principals with those considered to have something to offer, especially administratively, and who might donate money to the school as well). My first assignment was to P.S. 121. OMG. I have a photo of that too, where I am proudly standing in front of the school, surrounded by kids of color, wearing my recent wedding suit and tie, again put to good use. What I mostly remember from that day as "Principal" of 121 was entering the actual Principal's outer office where the secretaries sat, back then with their rotary phones and mechanical typewriters. At the far end of the space were foreboding doors that led to the Principal's office (and that of his leadership coterie). I looked at the high counter as I entered. My mind wandered back to being a student there. All I could think at that moment, as a grown man pretending to be principal, was my certain execution by the Vice Principal for having once again been caught in some piece of mischief.

It has been 60 years since I have played the accordion. I stopped sometime after elementary school—just lost interest I guess, or realized I was never going to get on TV. I gave away the one I had from that mid-town, Manhattan purchase decades ago when an inch of dust had settled upon it in a basement closet of my then Massachusetts home. Nowadays, my wife wants to get me one of those charming, small accordions they play, sometimes wearing berets, all around France. Who knows, maybe I will start again. If I do, at least you will be able to see me behind the instrument and it will be less to schlep around.

*****

4A: Music Among Youth

I have no idea what percentage of pre-teen kids have been shanghaied by their parents into playing a musical instrument or are the instigators themselves, like yours truly. Do you?

The list of instruments that accompany a youth's musical journey is long, but must be led by the guitar, drums, winds (clarinet, oboe), flute, strings (violin, cello, bass), brass (sax, trumpet, trombone), piano (though costlier to purchase and harder to store at home), or nowadays a keyboard. The recorder may top the list, but frankly, it should not count. Plus, instruments ancient and modern, from harmonicas small enough to grip in a palm to clavichords, harps and mammoth organs.

Note that I am not including voice: it is truly a wonder that music can come out full-throated with no hardware to help. The accordion, where this story began, is not high on such a list of frequently played instruments, France notwithstanding. It is sort of in a league with the mandolin or banjo, the xylophone, or chimes. I never said I was normative. But the accordion has to be more popular than playing the bagpipes or a dulcimer.

We all respond to music. While it enters our ears (sometimes the sound waves also can reverberate in our body, especially percussive instruments), it then travels to our brain's auditory processing centers (cortices), bilaterally. But it does not stop there. Circuits are fired touching off memory areas (like the hippocampus), and triggering associations there and in our frontal cortices. Rhythm engages our cerebellum, sitting as it does near to the bottom rear of the brain. We can "hear" (perhaps a different sensation applies) music in the womb. Music can and does alter how we feel; it can transport our minds to flights of fancy. We can be moved to tears. We can dissociate from everyday experience when listening to or making music. We can love or hate or simply not care about a piece of music. Clearly, loving is more desirable. Music is ubiquitous around the world and has been forever.

Why does one kid play an instrument and another not? Perhaps principally it is a matter of whether that child grows up in an environment, a family, that wants their child to have the pleasure (and discipline) it generates. It helps to have a family that can sponsor the costs and shoulder the time burden an instrument can require. In other words, it helps to come from a middle class (or more socially elevated) family. Poverty and domestic dysfunction don't help. 80% of the world's wealth is held by 20% of its population. Sometimes schools serve to introduce students to music, to playing an instrument or voice, but that has become uncommon today, especially in public schools, because of its budgetary impact. My parents, as far as I can recall, did not have "playing an instrument" on their list of expectations for me; mostly, it was good grades and civil behavior. Yet, I picked up the accordion; my sister, three years younger, was encouraged by our parents to play the piano, and an old upright arrived at our Bronx home.

Just about all kids listen to and are absorbed by music. Nowadays, it seems rare that a youth does not have earbuds piping in tunes; it is a kindness that their music is inaudible to others. But playing an instrument or developing voice is a different experience, I think, to simply listening. Too bad more kids don't have the chance. Making playing an instrument by a school (or a family) mandatory, not spawned by the youth's interests, can evoke contention, often leading to their abandonment of the effort. It takes support, work, and achieving the pleasure of mastery to sustain playing an instrument—all good things for that matter, seems to me. Playing and practicing an instrument helps the human brain to develop too.

My cousin Alan, from Queens, who is like a brother to me, is now living in Santa Monica, California. He is an attorney who manages the financial affairs of a small, highly successful group of people. One of those is Meredith Willson, now deceased, having left a foundation for music as one of his legacies. Alan is the President of the Meredith Willson Foundation.

Willson (1902-1984) was a gifted composer, arranger, and playwright (he also was a musician and bandleader). His exceptional success and legendary stature in entertainment came from his musical compositions and stage creations. His greatest show hit, for which he wrote the lyrics and music, was the Broadway musical, *The Music Man.* He also wrote *The Unsinkable Molly Brown*, another Broadway show that ran for two years, and was made into a film in 1964, starring Debbie Reynolds. Willson adapted the film *Miracle on 34th Street,* a Christmas standard, that was called *Here's Love* (1963). His music was twice nominated for Academy Awards. He and his wife, Rosemary, were great benefactors to The Julliard School of Music, where one building bears their name.

There is much more to Willson's musical bibliography, but I mention him (and my cousin) because of the work underway by the Meredith and Rosemary Willson Charitable Foundation. Its mission is to bring back music programs to public schools across the country—what had been publicly supported in the past, the likes of which I enjoyed, with so many other kids of my vintage.

In its work to date, this foundation is resurrecting music programs in public schools in Los Angeles and the metro-New York City area, so far. Its major recipient organization, which actually delivers the programs, is *Music Through Education* (https://etmla.org/about/). To become a "partner" school, music must become part of the core curriculum. Their ethos is that music enhances education, in its broadest ways: Children's music education has been linked to better reading, writing, and math skills. IQ increases of 7 points, as well, have been linked to the provision of music education, the effect lasting beyond the high school years. Music education also has been associated with greater self-confidence among those students who receive it. There are now 64 partner schools in the New York area, from Staten Island to Yonkers. Los Angeles has dozens.

The *Meeting Street Schools* in the Charleston, SC, area (https://meetingstreetschools.org/), exemplify enhancing the education and development of kids from under-resourced families and neighborhoods. The founders, Ben and Kelly Navarro, point out that youth from more privileged families are exposed to 38 million words, on average, by the time they enter elementary school, in contrast to 8 million words for kids less fortunate. Kids with more input into their brains and minds stand a better chance; those that do not are more likely to fall behind, prompting their feeling that they don't measure up.

Music, sports, and selected additional (and desired) subjects are coupled with longer school days and year-round attendance (though with more frequent breaks) at the *Meeting Street* schools. Families make a commitment to spend time with their child in reading and other enriching activities, or to volunteer at the school, ways by which they too are working to make a better life for the next generation. The results produced (and published on-line) by *Meeting Street Schools* demonstrate the value of their approach. But these schools are financed by philanthropy, a wonderful gift, though not apt to be "scaled up" (a great public health concept) to serve all the youth who could benefit, in South Carolina and throughout our country. Programs like this, however, can be leaders, showing the way for other schools and cities to follow.

Our brains are what is called "plastic." Reading, music, writing, sports, art, dance, drama, and other creative activities fashion more connections among our brain cells, creating new, additional, cerebral circuits. This means better neural wiring, not so different from how additional blood vessels grow in the heart from exercise. More areas of the brain work in synergy, faster too. The 100 billion brain cells we have function more optimally and their 1000 trillion (!) neural connections better harmonize in order to amplify our mental functioning.

But brain development, by whatever means, doesn't just happen passively. It takes work. Though that work can become its own source of pleasure. Playing a musical instrument (or training in voice), our primary example here, takes discipline, which itself is a means of enhancing cognition. How do you get to Julliard? As the joke goes: practice, practice, practice. Julliard connotes excellence, achievement, a super learning environment, and ever-increasing discipline and mastery. Of course, very few literally enter Julliard, though Jamie Foxx, (the actor) attended – no wonder he was superb playing in the film "Ray" (Charles). We know that these skills and acquired attributes can be achieved widely, replicated more broadly, but that too is not achieved passively; a person, family, community, school system, and government need to apply their collective shoulders to the wheel.

As amateur was my accordion playing, and I assure you it was, I learned to read music (a different language if you will), play a keyboard and bass buttons without looking (helped me learn to touch type, I think), and incorporate rhythm (good for the cerebellum, where our balance capabilities reside, aiding in sports, and good on the dance floor with girls!). And, over time, I was less alone, more connected to other kids by playing in a group, in my case an orchestra; for others, it will be a band, a duet, a quartet, and so on.

Still, I had to *practice*. To develop patience because any complex skill comes incrementally and slowly. I also needed the support of my family, protected time, money for (modest) expenses, and a school that had not been stripped of music education (or dance or sports). I was fortunate, as were many others, to grow up in a culture that valued music because there were those who loved it and appreciated that it promoted the cognitive, psychological, and social development of a child. Music is an amazing channel to all kinds of feelings, including joy, hurt, anger, wonder, sadness, inspiration, victory and defeat, a call to arms or battle, pride in the neighborhood (or region), ethnicity and country, and hope. Yet, most of all, acquiring the capacity to produce music can be a source of pleasure, for you and for those who take the time and interest to listen to what you play or sing.

*****

Chapter 5
Running Away from Home

I must have been nine or ten, thereabouts, since that's when parents let—or wish to have—their boys completely creep out of their sights, unsupervised. To do what kids want to do and when parents don't want to be pestered. My best friend was my cousin, Steve, a few months older than me— the older son of my mother's sister, Muriel. They lived in Queens, Forest Hills (near where the tennis stadium is now), but it was as if they lived next door to us, since we saw them about every weekend, and spent summers together on my uncle's (hobby) chicken farm in Walden, New York, in Orange County, near the Catskill Mountains.

My grandparents, Rose and JT, on my mother's side, lived with us, in the ground floor apartment of our brick, three-decker, attached house on the corner of Eastchester Road and Hammersley Avenue, which pitched violently downhill and east towards the Long Island Sound. In the '50s, *Freedom Land,* a vast amusement park (an east coast *Disneyland* wannabe about the same time the Anaheim version first sprouted) was at the very bottom of the hill. That fizzled and died. Now we have Route 95.

My grandparents were immigrants from Eastern Europe, and my grandmother worked in her brother-in-law's antique store on the Bowery. So, her home (really more like an apartment) had antiques, like furniture, lamps, paintings, and *chatzkes*.

Steve and I were watching TV one weekend afternoon, having escaped to our grandparents' ground floor apartment from upstairs—where our parents (and grandparents) were gathered, talking, smoking too. We started horsing around, wrestling with each other. We must have kicked one of the side tables because next thing we knew, a lamp had crashed to the floor, shattered. We immediately knew we would soon be labeled menaces to society, as soon as our parents discovered the lamp's destruction.

I think it was my idea about what to do: to run away, even though I would like to blame Steve for the idea. We would escape the unjust punishment ahead (which we had coming), was what I think I must have advanced to Steve as a solution. Not to mention that our having gone missing would surely inspire solicitous attention, even indulgence, from our mothers. We also could exert our fledgling independence, I guess imagining back. The weather was warm, it wasn't raining, and we weren't hungry, we had already eaten lunch.

We slipped out the ground-floor door next to the garage and headed north on Eastchester Road, soon crossing the trestle, the bridge over the train tracks below, a Rubicon it felt. We reached Boston Post Road, a great thoroughfare with lots of stores, even a movie theatre. We wanted to buy something to eat, like ice cream or candy, but we had no money. We lamented and were sorry for ourselves, the street urchins we had become. In a desultory way, we wandered more north, not much, since that was totally new to me. We entered apartment building territory, scared a bit since any kind of ill-tempered person could live there. The side-streets were quiet but boring—just lots of houses and parked cars.

We presumed, or at least I tried to convince Steve, that they (our parents) would surely be aggrieved by our loss. We wandered for about another hour, then decided to go home. We had no place to go except there, and it was getting dark. We shuffled back to 3100 Eastchester Road and braced for the reception we now feared we would receive. We didn't expect trumpets to be playing.

My and Steve's mom both first issued a sigh of relief: We hadn't been kidnapped or killed, a good thing, I guess, because who could pay any ransom, and the cost of the funerals could be prohibitive. Then they got mad. Not just for the lamp, which turned out not to be a real antique, but for running away and creating the awful mother's fear we did. Our crime jumped from the misdemeanor of a playful, unintended accident to the felony of creating maternal fear about the fate of their sons. I knew my aunt wanted to hit us with a wooden spoon like she would from time to time (though we usually eluded her swing). But she wasn't in her own kitchen and my mother didn't hit, just wore you down with questions and guilt. It might have been better to be hit since that might have felt less painful than their disappointment with us. Then came their long talk with us (it was probably minutes but felt like days in captivity). They both let us know that we should have understood the worry we would create doing such a dumb thing, especially me, said Muriel, I recall, since I was supposed to be the really smart kid in the family.

No more TV that weekend. Scowls everywhere we went. Then my aunt and cousins went back to Queens. The whole episode faded away at our home, or maybe I have buried the recollection among the many painful memories of what has been my less than decorous life. I was clearly no angel. The very next weekend, I saw my aunt, Muriel. She greeted me heartily in her crowded Queens kitchen. No wooden spoon came of the drawer, to be wielded against me in the old-fashioned way of making a point. She gave me her million-dollar smile. She was one of the most beautiful women I had ever seen.

*****

5A: Boys Will Be Boys

I was visiting a friend's home; she and her husband had two children. A girl about six and a boy about four. I love kids and sometimes ignore my adult hosts to play with them. These two lively, wide-eyed children invited me to look at their rooms, evidently sources of pride.

We went to Nora's room first. Pastel colors, tidy, and replete with about every type of doll ever marketed to girls, and their adoring parents. I was duly impressed and said so. Then we moved on to her brother Joe's room. As we approached the door, Nora said to me, "don't be afraid but his room is full of weapons." Indeed, it was: ray guns, swords, water pistols, and tiny cannons to equip his collection of toy soldiers. Of course, there were plenty of toy trucks of every stripe (dozers, dump trucks, backhoes, you get the picture), cars, fire engines, and locomotives. Clothes were strewn here and there, and stuff cluttered on every available surface.

Day and night. Girls and boys are different; not always but I would be a rich man from the odds if I could bet on the difference. Even in families like this one, with two professional parents and a deep sense of parity between the sexes.

The differences are not just with their rooms and possessions. Girls are more disposed to relationships. Their verbal abilities usually mature sooner than boys. Boys are more action-oriented, and when older tend to put more of a premium on performance than on people. Girls have different color preferences, as a rule, though my friend, the writer Andrew Solomon, a gay man, points out that when he was a boy, he picked pink over blue and had no use for trucks or weapons, preferring the scores and librettos of operas. Of course, these differences among the sexes are generalizations; yet, again, the odds are with me in case you want to lose some money over a series of bets.

In other words, boys will be boys and girls will be girls—most of the time. My cousin Steve and I were boys—back in the days when the XY chromosome pair was given special standing and opportunity (not that we have yet to achieve equality between the sexes, even in this country). We had been wrestling in our grandparents' apartment, broke a lamp, and ran away. Just like the impulsive boys we were. Not a thought about how others, like our parents and grandparents, might feel to discover us missing.

My psychoanalyst, many years ago, was Dr. Gregory Rochlin of Cambridge, Massachusetts. I frequented his couch four times a week for six long years (worth it!). He was a wise man, now long deceased, a child psychiatrist, and a child analyst as well. He specialized in boys, which gave him an unfair advantage with me, especially since I didn't want to grow up. I liked being an unruly boy.

One book he wrote was about how boys are different. I bought it back then, seeking to better level the playing field in his office. He did not think boys better, just generally different—a useful distinction when rearing or teaching children. Or analytically treating men who acted more like boys.

Please let me be clear that population or individually based differences do not, and should not limit any person, woman or man, from achieving success in work or relationships. Even physically: For the first time in history, women are graduating from Army Ranger training where strength and endurance are exceedingly challenged. But differences exist and need to be understood if we are to be most equitable.

MRI and other highly sensitive imaging (e.g., PET scanning) of the brain, for example, including scientific reports of cerebral volume and circuits, reveal sex differences—as do hormonal studies of the sexes. They may have implications for developing and delivering gender-specific approaches to a number of mental health conditions, including depression, PTSD, substance use disorders, and psychotic conditions like schizophrenia. While what we know about the brain, cognition, feelings, and behavior remains very rudimentary (and may change its theories as the march of science is wont to do), social scientists and educated readers need to keep an open mind about what we know and can do today.

For example, fetuses with XY chromosomes (boys) are exposed in utero to far higher levels of male hormones (especially testosterone, as well as vasopressin and Müllerian Inhibiting Substance, MIS) as early as nine weeks; levels peak again in puberty and are far greater than in those with XX chromosomes (girls). In contrast, females produce very different levels of estrogen, progesterone, and oxytocin (the bonding and "cuddling" hormone). Testosterone and other androgens influence brain development in several ways. Greater exposure to androgens is associated with differences in brain regions like the amygdala (the fear center and where emotional memory can be formed); the hippocampus (which influences learning and long-term memory); parts of the prefrontal cortex (associated with judgment and control). There also is evidence of variations in gray matter (cells) brain volume between the sexes.

One result is that manual and cognitive skills can differ between boys and girls. Males (even monkeys not exposed to cultural influences as are humans) selectively prefer toys like trucks that can be moved through space and that lend themselves to activity, including gross physical movements. Males prefer different colors than females. Females do better than males in tests that measure recollection as well as in more precision motor tasks. There are also differences in behaviors consistent with many of the brain differences described above. Empathy, which is higher on average in females than males, can be reduced by exposure to testosterone in utero. There is a genetic condition, congenital adrenal hyperplasia, that increases male hormone production beginning before birth, which is associated with reduced empathy.

In a very funny yet smart website called *Man Therapy,* we see the site host seeking comfort by holding a tape recorder to his ear that plays the revving sounds of a big-engine car. Other parts of the site are more serious but may not be more revealing regarding a man's nature.

Stress responses, as well, can be different between the sexes. These may relate to the amygdala and the hippocampus, as well as to neurotransmitters like serotonin. Females may be more resilient than males when faced with chronic stress, which we know to be a factor in developing many psychiatric and medical illnesses including depression, PTSD, hypertension, diabetes, dementia, and autoimmune disorders.

Addictions (substance use disorders) appear highly linked with brain dopamine, the "pleasure" or reward neurotransmitter. There are notable differences in dopamine levels in people who develop addictions. There are changes in this neurotransmitter's activity after exposure to substances of abuse like cocaine, stimulants, and ecstasy—as well as in behavioral addictions like gambling and video games. Dopamine and its release may be increased by estrogen, possibly making females more at risk for addiction. These differences suggest psychotherapeutic treatment approaches that may be different for men and women.

Females, as well, may have greater prefrontal cortex volume, especially in the ratio of the size of the cortex to the size of the amygdala area of the brain. This may provide females with more capacity for behavior control; it suggests using cognitive and motivational psychotherapy approaches when problem behaviors occur. This finding of greater brain volume, as well, may be present in people with schizophrenia, and make for different presentations and course of the illness in women than men.

Gray (cells) and white (connective tissue) brain tissue sex differences are salient because white matter provides connectivity for cells and among brain regions. Differences in their volume may account for why females are better multi-taskers and why males do better on highly task-oriented activities. Words mean more to females than males, again, in general, which may relate to their larger bilateral verbal brain centers. These differences may help in thinking about and fashioning cognitive and other psychotherapy approaches.

Extending what we know from brain science and public mental health into everyday practice is critical—but often not an easy or small step.

Cognitive approaches in therapy, for example, need to consider different mental skill sets among men and women. Men are drawn to solving problems, especially those that require motor and spatial skills; how can we use that in gaining their attention and trust in therapy? Targeting neurotransmitters, by various methods including hormonal administration, to produce beneficial results will need to consider what is known of their differences between the sexes. The need for men to contain feelings and protect against shame related to feeling inferior, "not quite a man," may be ingrained in the amygdala and hippocampus and thus will need the "right" approach. A good example was offered in The Opinion Pages of the New York Times in *Therapy for Tough Guys* (August 4, 2015), where an informed therapist knew that "touchy-feely" was not going to work with the macho man who sought his help.

Evolutionary biologists and geneticists will remind us that differences are not only important; they are essential for species survival and adaptation. *Vive La Différence*, may, in fact, be quite right in saluting (in this case gender) differences. When differences do exist, they need to be recognized, understood, and used to help manage everyday life as well as in fashioning therapies with greater clinical precision and utility.

It's been over six decades since my cousin Steve and I ran away from home. As much as I have learned, grown up (matured may be an exaggeration), and come to believe in a world where sex differences are real but hugely varied and mutable, I fear that I remain a boy at heart. Yet because of the residual boy buried in my man's body, I have tried to layer on empathy, consider others, live with a deep belief in the power of relationships and attachment, and to practice gratitude. It has taken, however, a lifetime full of painful moments to promote those changes.

*****

Chapter 6
The Twerys

You could ride a bicycle around their kitchen, a small bike I grant you but, still, one with only two wheels. Though, not one like they use in *La Tour de France*. I swear it was true because I remember getting yelled at for doing just that, bicycling circles around the gigantic, wooden table in the center of the room.

Their home was a mansion in Tarrytown, New York. Right next to where the Rockefellers had their estate. Yes, a property abutting the Rockefellers, American nobility. Near Sleepy Hollow, NY, where the Headless Horseman could get you. I wonder if the real estate agent, back then, revealed to the local *gentiles* that Jews were buying the property?

The Twery mansion was a massive stone fortress of a home. Formidable, fit to repel barbarians, with an immense, steel gray, slate roof sheltering its three (maybe four) stories, not counting the dark, terrifying basement. As improbable as it was, that was where Abe and Eva Twery lived. At least when I was a boy. Tante Eva was my grandma (on my mother's side) Rose's older sister. Uncle Abe and Tante Eva were immigrants from Eastern Europe at the turn of the 20th century. Abe Twery had owned and had built a very successful, large (almost a city block wide), two-level, dingy, and *ungapatchka'd* (Yiddish for terribly busy, deeply disorganized, and yet functional) antique store on the Bowery.

I had been to the store a bit since Grandma Rose worked there, and her husband, my grandpa JT, sold men's clothing nearby at an upper scale men's store, also on the Lower East Side of Manhattan. The former Twery antique store today has become a huge lighting outlet, which still sells chandeliers (but mostly more modern fixtures) and every type of light bulb on earth. I don't know what my grandmother did at the antique store, but she didn't do sales. She was a bit dour, shy, humble. But she also was very determined, a hard worker, totally loyal. She was close— trusted family to Abe and Eva. Of course, she would do *anything* for her two daughters, my mother and her younger sister, Muriel, and even more for her grandchildren, like me.

The Twerys went to "Europe" a lot. I thought, at first, they must have been up to something nefarious. What did I know from my tiny perch in the Bronx? Sometime later, I found out they went to buy old (antique—read expensive) oil paintings, lamps and chandeliers, furniture, and *chatzkes* (surely you know what these are)—so many of these items that they had to be shipped back to New York in massive metal cartons, loaded onto Transatlantic ships. Somehow, Uncle Abe had realized, by the 1950s, the immigrant's dream of going from nothing to becoming a (antique) magnate. The Twerys must have known where to go abroad to buy, gotten great bargains, and bought low and sold high, because they became rich. Rich, like they had so much money, as I discovered, they could (and did) buy a mansion in Tarrytown, next to you know who.

I have, hanging in our NYC apartment, one large British-school waterfall painting, a smaller barn scene with a boy and animals (that hung in my room as a child), and two small, ornately framed landscapes, all from the 19th century. My sister has a small collection as well. Thanks to our grandma Rose, and the Bowery store, where she must have been paid, in part, with art.

Grandma Rose and JT lived on the ground floor of our Bronx, attached brick house. Tante Eva had arranged her marriage to JT when they both were new to New York City. JT had come down from Canada where he first emigrated to escape the pogroms in the Ukraine. Rose took the train way down into Lower Manhattan to the antique store five or six days a week, packing a simple lunch wrapped in a brown paper bag for herself and Abe, like outreach workers give to homeless people. At first, I figured Abe must have been even poorer than my grandmother for her to have to feed him. Then I saw his mansion.

We went to visit Tarrytown because Tante Eva had a daughter, Bertha, who grew up with my mother and her sister Muriel. These three girls were really close, bonded like epoxy, as their mothers (new to this country) were sisters and refugees from the nightmares of their Eastern European past. Bertha, who also then lived in NYC, of course regularly visited her parents, Abe and Eva, not just at the shop on the Bowery but at their home, the mansion. And when she did, she usually brought her son, Scott, a name for a Jew as unusual in the '40s as Lloyd was. Scott was the same age as my cousin Steve (Muriel's first son, and my best friend) and me. It was a time for the boys, first and second cousins, to get together and play at the estate in Tarrytown.

We didn't go there very often. It was far from the Bronx and Queens. It seemed foreign, for us almost like going abroad, not that we knew how that felt. Steve and I thought Scott was spoiled, selfish. We were barely ten and he had a motorized, little car he would drive up and down their endless driveway. He wouldn't let us get in the contraption, certainly not permit us to take the wheel. And he had more toys than *FAO Schwartz*, especially toy soldiers, which I coveted. There was a swimming pool behind the house, reached by a gentle downward slope of perfect lawn that also led to the clay tennis court. I never saw Uncle Abe or Tante Eva use the tennis court or the pool. They liked to look out over them from the house. Neither Steve, Scott, or I played tennis, not a sport back then for Jewish kids of modest, outer-borough means, but we did like the pool. And Steve and I secretly explored the vast house, like in a scary movie—usually upon my instigation, I admit.

Uncle Abe also was a regular visitor to my grandma's home. She was like a caretaker to him, especially as he aged. He would come up to the small, simple apartment where she and JT lived, on the ground floor of our Bronx house. He would take a nap late in the day or sometimes stay to have dinner, which Rose prepared. He never stayed over. Rose never stopped packing lunches for Abe. Then one afternoon, when I was a young teenager, he didn't wake up from resting in the basement apartment of our home. I recall going downstairs after it was clear he had died in his sleep. It was like a tomb down there. A black hearse came to take him away. That was the end of Tarrytown, for them and for us. Bertha, Eva, and their family moved to Florida.

I guess they sold the antique store since Grandma Rose stopped packing bag lunches and schlepping downtown. And the Tarrytown mansion too; I never went there again. The end of my Great Gatsby wannabe era.

I returned to New York City in 2002 to live and work, having left 36 years earlier after my college graduation. Once again, I was a true New Yorker; even my mother was happy, and she lived in Florida. One fall day, with a bright sun to illuminate my search, I decided to drive to Tarrytown. It was hard to find where they had lived. But I approximated its location, having looked up the old Rockefeller estate. I drove around the neighborhood. The Twery property had been subdivided, many a time. There were lots of big homes, but no mansion. It must have been torn down.

*****

6A: Rich People

We all know the old saw about rich people, attributed to an exchange between Fitzgerald and Hemingway. To paraphrase, they are different, they have money.

But rich people are as varied as species of birds or gerbils, except of course they are hominids. As a boy, my parents and relatives used to talk about rich people in hushed tones, with a reverence befitting saints, even though we were not Catholics. They were not just different, awash in money, they had special standing in the scheme of things.

It was as if they stood as beacons for what it meant to have made it in this country, the new world for most of my family, and for what they aspired to achieve, especially my father. He believed that being rich brought social standing and more than warranted, almost demanded, respect. For first-generation Jews, like my parents, money was the path to assimilation and the signifier of success.

There are three ways to get rich: inheritance, earning wealth (aka working, sometimes with good luck thrown in), and stealing. The last one, being a *goniff* (a Yiddish word often used in my home), has been around probably longer than the others. Aside from any moral imperatives, it's not a good idea to steal since sooner or later you are apt to get caught; that brings misfortune of all sorts, though has not proven much of a deterrent over time.

Inheriting money may appear the most fortunate means of becoming wealthy. But wealth does not assure good fortune, if you know what I mean. As a psychiatrist, I have seen too many rich people ablate their abundance by a life of unmitigated dissolution, often associated with a want of purpose or meaning. Still, being an heir, especially having a sizable trust fund, is nothing to sneeze at. Over time, in this country, the passage of wealth from one generation to the next has become easier, with greater amounts possible, thanks to smart lawyers and newer, federal IRS codes.

Acquiring money, going from little to enough is usually done the old-fashioned way, by earning it (as an investment company once advertised). It needs saying that being of a person of color, born into a variety of ethnicities, having a lower economic status, without access to good education, and domestic instability can foreclose earning a livable wage, no less being rich. Not fair or just, which needs to be said again and again. Finally, luck always has its uncertain role, since being in the right place—for example living during eras of growth and prosperity—is often happenstance, how the roll of the dice lands.

If, by the way, you know of a fourth way to get rich, please be in touch with me. The sooner the better. Maybe don't tell anyone else until you have told me how.

Rich *goyim* (Yiddish for non-Jews, usually not in the most complimentary manner), were almost impossible for us to emulate. It was not just their wealth, but their manners, their privileged, private education, and their class. Some were the "old rich," usually American settlers who early on had been pirates or financial titans, like those who now live on Park Avenue or facing Central Park, in New York City, or in Marblehead on the Massachusetts shoreline. Many had "second homes," an understatement compared to the totally adequate but modest home we had. This summer place, or just a weekend escape from the city, often was in Connecticut or Quogue (wherever that may be).

Then there were those who came to be known as the "*nouveau riche*," having obtained great business success and wealth during the 20th (and now 21st) century. They were rich, but newly so, and did not evoke the same reverence as the old rich. They also were different, having amassed vast capital from being there at the start in companies like Google, Apple, and Amazon, or by selling a tech startup to a bigger fish up the food chain. These more recent billionaires, not merely millionaires like their predecessors, are hugely rich; it is if they are made of 21-carat gold.

John D. Rockefeller was the richest American of the 20th century. His fortune was not from land or banks but from oil, having ruled Standard Oil, which back then controlled 90% (!) of the earth's petroleum production. Even when this massive, global corporation was forced to split into over 30 separate companies, that transaction substantially increased Rockefeller's wealth. Go figure.

There were, of course, the Kennedys. Joseph P. Kennedy Sr. was the founder of that American elite clan and its patriarch. His fortune was amassed in finance, playing a dominant role in the world of securities and banks. Among the Kennedys have been two ambassadors, a senator who became a president, an attorney general, another senator, and some congressmen, not counting more local elected or appointed positions. They had *noblesse oblige.*

There also was the Hearst family, who began their rise with newspapers and then became oligarchs in radio and television. Remember the great film, *Citizen Kane*?

Emanating economic royalty, while still being Jewish, were the Rothschilds, originally German bankers whose hegemony in the finance world spread to Britain, then throughout Europe, and subsequently into the New World.

Of course, there were many others, but I hope these examples, many with their storied or Camelot lives, almost boundless power, and bottomless bank accounts, give you a sense of the bigger-than-life shadows they cast, especially in the minds of the immigrants and aspiring members in the middle-class.

The lot of rich Jewish people continued to grow, especially after World War II. Their wealth usually came from owning businesses and growing corporations, small and large, or from investing, as the 20th century evolved. These included fabled men like Soros, Bloomberg, and Lauder. They occupied a very respectable league of their own, unattainable to families like mine; but my parents' generation could ponder, could they get close?

In addition to the Twerys, in my life was Max Low, a customer in my father's Westchester stationery business. Mr. Low had made his fortune in the hospital supply business, operating one of the largest of its sort in the country, called IPCO Hospital Supply. He was an elegant man, short, with a kindly manner, who had not lost sight of his roots, or the road Jews needed to make in America. When I worked in the family stationery store, continuing my indentured service there as a teenager (on weekends, the times I thought I should be free), he would religiously come in early on Saturday and Sunday mornings, to buy the newspapers, and occasional sundries. My father regularly got into a conversation with him; my best guess was that it was about business or the stock market. I knew my father thought Mr. Low walked on water, sacred water of the Jewish kind. Later, as I will tell in the story titled *Savin Business Machines*, he would become a channel for me to graduate from my family's business and enter a bigger world.

The Twerys were an anomaly. Not many like them, I think. Modest looking Jews, they lived like misers despite their mansion, antique and art collection, and money. They didn't drive big, expensive sedans. Abe, the patriarch, ate the bag lunch that my grandmother, his sister-in-law, made for him, daily, and brought on the subway from the Bronx to the Bowery, where the antique store was located. The

Twerys did not book passage to Europe on the Queen Elizabeth, though they no longer went steerage, as they had when they first came west. Uncle Abe, as I knew him, dressed in discount, though good quality clothes, selected for him by my dapper grandfather, the men's "haberdasher" who knew how to hawk passersby, working at G & Gs, on Stanton Street, also on the Lower East Side of New York.

I imagine the Twerys psychologically never fully left behind their Eastern European village, their hardscrabble pasts. What had come into them to buy the Tarrytown property, fit for a Rockefeller, I never understood, back then or now. They also never spread their wealth beyond their children, or used it for a common good, with philanthropic giving. I don't know if they even gave to their Shul. They lived an insular existence, uneducated and perhaps sensing that their manners and edification were too far from the social circles of the wealthy Jews and non-Jews that surrounded them.

John Gardner remarked, "Wealth is not new. Neither is charity. But the idea of using private wealth imaginatively, constructively, and systematically to attack the fundamental problems of mankind is new."

The term philanthropy derives from Greek and means love of or kindliness to mankind (sic). The earliest forms of philanthropy, aside from helping thy neighbor, were religious in nature. Giving to a church, for example, by a tithe was everyone's responsibility, though meant to be a moral obligation. Prosperous landowners and merchants in the Middle Ages also sought mercy and recognition from their generous donations to their respective religious orders.

It was the growth of cities and the emergence of a more secular culture that gave new meaning to giving.

By the end of the 1800s, wars in Europe and the United States left societies with legions of widows, orphans, and infirm. There were many displaced from homes and cities. The Industrial Revolution began a march to more material comforts, but also created horrendous conditions from working in factories and living in tenements and city slums. The value and quality of human lives more than ever needed to become more of a societal concern and was given life through movements for workers' rights. A responsibility to aid the less fortunate emerged; local and national government support was not sufficient to meet the needs of the vast numbers of people ground down by poverty and ill health. It was not until the mid-30s of the 20th century that Social Security was introduced in this country; it took thirty more years to pass legislation (thank you, Lyndon Baines Johnson) that established Medicare and Medicaid, making health care, which had become prohibitively expensive, possible for seniors, the disabled, and the poor.

The turn of the 20th century had brought further prosperity, and with it the opportunity to spread the wealth. Andrew Carnegie had offered a *Gospel of Wealth*, calling for the redistribution of money concentrated in the rich to those far less fortunate, as well as for the public good. Captains of industry, such as Carnegie and others, founded private foundations for giving, which brought discipline to what often had become self-serving and unaccountable in earlier, non-religious, charitable contributions.

Philanthropy, by the mid-20th century, especially after World War II, also then aimed to respond to the surging needs of veterans and civilians living in war-ravaged economies and failing cities. A growing ethos of human and civil rights added momentum to giving to those who were less fortunate, for reasons beyond their control. Philanthropies spawned at community levels, with their more local missions and discrete populations to serve.

Today, we see quite amazing, global philanthropies and philanthropists, many endowed by family wealth like that of Gates, Rockefeller, Buffett, Bloomberg, Hughes, Soros, MacArthur, and Pew. The Sackler family, of New York, were great patrons of medical centers, the opera, and museums, but then came their ignominy. Their fortune was principally amassed from their drug company, Purdue Pharmaceuticals, which made billions selling and distributing OxyContin, the opioid pain pill that they contended was not addicting—which, of course, it was, and which was a powerful fuel for the opioid epidemic that then seized this country.

Many philanthropies are corporately financed, not-for-profit creations of their parent for-profit companies. These global philanthropies have missions focused on health, economic vitality, education, women's rights, and victims of natural disasters; some fund technological advances. A quantitative method, with roots in the concept of "return on investment," now dominates the practices of most successful charities, where specific—and measurable—aims must be proposed to determine if funding will be provided. If an award, a grant, is given, it is followed with careful, ongoing monitoring that assesses if these purported goals are being achieved. The recipients of varied philanthropies, whether people in need, health and scientific experts, or social entrepreneurs, have now, also, themselves begun to serve roles in the governance, on the Boards, of philanthropies, and in so doing help to shape future policies and programs, as well as their successful execution.

Rich people often, but not always, are given to "paying forward," the concept that when we are the beneficiaries of good fortune, literally and figuratively, we should use that wealth to give others a chance. Philanthropies, not only big ones, become experts in obtaining donations from prosperous donors as well as those of modest means—those with an emotional stake in the enterprise and its sought-after outcomes. Tax benefits, deductions, as well, have accrued to those companies and individuals—in this country—who share their wealth, though there has been an erosion of these incentives because of federal regulatory limitations.

Not all nations or cultures are well disposed to charitable giving. China and India are among the lowest ranking, large national givers. Australia, New Zealand, and Ireland are among the leaders, not in money but in the percentage of people who give. The United States and the UK are not far behind on this latter measure. Because many foundations and philanthropies cross national boundaries, ranking countries by philanthropic assets and donations has become an elusive enterprise.

Among wealthy families, there also is a long history of public service. Positions often have been held by the rich and famous as elected and appointed officials in municipal, county, state and federal government, in diplomatic posts, on not-for-profit Boards, and as emissaries of peace and health. Some of us are just good old, public servants, without family fortunes but privileged to take on the mantle of societal responsibility, even at government wages. But for many who serve on the global stage, in diplomacy, government, or healthcare, it has been their self-made or family wealth and sense of charity that has fostered a life of public service, and, for some, the capital to support such a livelihood, especially those seeking political success.

I don't know quite how I lost my appetite for making money, at least bundles of it; for being a businessman and hopefully amassing wealth. Not that I don't like the benefits – and security – that money can provide. Instead, I was, like many a good Jewish boy, shaped to be a doctor, while others of my generation entered less lucrative fields and became teachers, scientists, engineers, nurses and (god forbid) musicians, dancers, and artists.

My father was fine with my entering the medical field, but hugely disappointed, truly, when I began training to be a psychiatrist, instead of becoming a surgeon (where I would have more respect and earn a lot more money, he believed). During my psychiatric residency—I kid you not—he offered to lend me (not give me) money so I could switch out of my psychiatric residency and go into general surgery, neurosurgery, ophthalmology, even orthopedics. As you can see, I didn't take him up on the offer, and can't recall what interest rate he expected from his loan.

All that said, the Twerys were my earliest, first-hand experience of wealth. They were not prototypical, so I discovered. But I will never forget the size of their kitchen.

*****

Chapter 7
Orchard Street I

My grandfather, JT, didn't want to die. Can't blame him. I feel the same way. So as a young man, around the turn of the 20th century, he left his parents and his native country, Ukraine, when the pogroms were in full flower. He fled to Canada, booking steerage on a steamer, the kind of ship you see in old documentaries.

JT, short for Jacob (or Jack) Travis, had relatives in Winnipeg, the capital of Manitoba – and Canada's then third-largest city, at 272,000 registered inhabitants. It was geographically perilously close to Hudson Bay, which we know is a channel to the Arctic, the North Pole not being a very friendly place for those who are not explorers. I imagine the men of Winnipeg preferred practical wool clothing, not the silk or gaberdine suits and jackets that would become my grandfather's livelihood and trademark.

Winnipeg turned out to be no match for Kyiv, the cosmopolitan capital of Ukraine, a historic city, with a population of about 250,000 people, where JT had lived before he had to escape. Winnipeg had become a North American haven for Jews, where distant relatives offered shelter to Eastern European *landsmen* (countrymen) needing to flee for their lives or overcome the opportunities foreclosed to them because they were Jews. I don't think Winnipeg then had a shul. But all you need are ten men, a *minyan*, and a Hebrew prayer service can proceed.

Winnipeg also was not New York City, that's for sure, where other Ukrainians had entered (and stayed on) in North America. NYC was (still is) a magnificent large city and the "center of the universe" to many, which is where JT evidently wanted to be. He liked fine suits and ties—and cufflinks. He had style, was a dapper guy, a talker too. He didn't last long in Winnipeg. There were connections in New York City and he made his way to Ellis Island and then onto Manhattan Island, another crucial step into a bigger, more promising life. He made the Lower East Side his home, where he lived in a tenement among fellow Jews, as well as plenty of Irish and German immigrants. He got a job at G & G Clothiers, a men's clothing store on Stanton Street, which sold brand-name, high(er)-quality suits, pants, and ties at lower east-side prices. First, he was the guy standing in front of the shop, all day, whose job was to lure easy marks into the store, where someone else would take over. While his English, at first, was pretty limited, he spoke Yiddish, the native tongue of lower east-side Jews.

Then he worked his way inside. He became a men's haberdasher. What a great word. Every morning, Tuesday through Saturday, he would dress up in the ground floor apartment of our Eastchester Road home, catch the IRT at Gun Hill Road and work his way to the lower east-side. Rose, his wife, my grandmother, had no patience for his dressing so well and spending what little money he earned on clothes, even if they were discounted. She dressed in *shmatas*, house dresses, and made her own lunch, not his. She too, daily, worked her way down into Lower Manhattan, to the Bowery, not so far from JT in distance but miles away in their everyday existence. They had an arranged marriage through Rose's sister, pretty common at the time. My father thought that JT was a bit of a light-weight, a judgment my dad was prone to make, but my mother, his daughter, loved him dearly, as did I.

He had *joie de vivre,* a joy for life. I treasured time with him, to hear him tell stories about the big and little shots he met at G & G. About the food and energy and kaleidoscope of people this cherished lower eastside neighborhood of his provided, so different from Eastchester Road. JT liked to embellish his tales. That made them all the better, even when—or maybe more—his wife frowned.

Then one day, I guess when I was ten, well before my Bar Mitzvah (which would call for another trip to the lower east-side), he took me on a Saturday to G & G. On Shabbos, no less. When we left our house, he looked like he was going to an inauguration, in his dark, tailored suit and flecked tie. My grandfather, the haberdasher, was going to dress me in a sports jacket, pants, and a white shirt and tie, which I would get to bring home (after alterations). We got on the elevated subway on Gun Hill Road, which snaked through the Bronx and entered Northern Manhattan, finally going underground. We had to have transferred trains, but it was a blur to me.

We finally got to the Lower East Side, emerging from the underground subway, and made our way to the store. JT proudly entered. He introduced me to the other men, who made a big deal of this little Jewish kid from the Bronx.

They had that baloney down, used it day in and day out with everybody who walked in, no doubt. I, too, was in their commercial cross-hairs that day, even though JT would get the clothes for wholesale. There were racks and racks of suits, jackets, and pants—for men and boys. Every color imaginable, some smart and some awful. You needed a map to know where to go, but JT knew the place by heart.

He picked out what we would buy, with some automatic nodding on my part. Then an older man, more plainly dressed, with a cloth tape measure hanging around his neck reaching to his belt on both sides, emerged from the back. He did the tailoring, the alterations. I don't think he spoke any English. He made chalk marks on my pants—the behind, legs, and cuffs—and in the back of the jacket and on its sleeves. The shirt was my size, the blue tie too, so we could leave with those. I think we went to Ratner's, the kosher, dairy restaurant nearby, for blintzes, but that may have been another Saturday on the Lower East Side. Our memories are imperfect, especially for little things.

There would be Bar and Bat Mitzvahs to go to, maybe a wedding, no funerals back then. And I could be all dressed up, thanks to JT and his impeccable eye for clothes. From the time I finished my psychiatric residency and was making some money as a young doctor, I loved to buy clothing and to dress up like a New Yorker, which didn't go over that much in Boston, where I had started working at the Massachusetts General Hospital. But I didn't care, I was going to be an outsider there no matter what I did. I was the only service chief in my department who had not been born and raised in the Harvard system. I did, however, last six years at MGH before I moved on, professionally, to Cambridge, Massachusetts.

I first bought clothes retail in Boston. But that was way too expensive. Then I discovered a men's store run by Argentinian, Hassidic Jews on Grand Street, in New York City. They were closed on Friday night and Saturday, Shabbos. They sold designer brands like Hugo Boss, Versace, Brioni, and others, but not Armani in case you want to know. At about 40% of retail, and no charge for alterations. I still go there every few years, less and less now, since I am more interested in skinny khakis and sneakers (which I learned from Charlie Rose, who wore sneakers all the time—except when he interviewed the President of some country; I don't know if he still does, after his fall from grace).

After JT died, which he did when my parents were still living on Eastchester Road, my mother asked me if I wanted to look through JT's clothing and take what I wanted. She knew I had the bug for nice clothes, just like he did. I was in medical school and had come down to the City for the funeral. After the *Shiva*, the Jewish mourning ritual, I went downstairs on Eastchester Road to where he and grandma Rose (who had also passed) lived. It felt like a morgue—a strangely familiar place since I then was in medical school.

There were closets bursting with his clothes: suits, sports jackets, pants, shirts, ties, and accessories. Some were dated, out of style. I guess he wasn't in the habit of giving them away. Yet some were gorgeous, reflecting the closet light off their fine cloth. But they didn't fit. He was smaller than me, by at least 4 inches, and I was pretty thin back then too. There was nothing to do but leave them for the Salvation Army. I took some ties, handfuls of socks, and a couple of pairs of cufflinks.

They were my treasure. I still have the cuff links.

*****

7A: Clothing, if Not Fashion

I don't know if clothing "makes the man" or the woman. But clearly, clothing is far more than the vestments we wear to protect us from the cold and the wet or to maintain some measure of public decency. My report below must be seen as applying to white men of the 1950s, of which I am one, of middle-class (sometimes higher) socio-economic status. A limited view, for sure, since so many people of modest means and varied ethnicities populated this country. So, please forgive me.

Clothing is a huge industry, and fashion in women's and men's wear has become a high, and very costly, form of expression. In the '50s, as I came of age and when I began to visit Orchard Street for clothing, men (at business or professional settings) typically wore suits or sports jackets. Big lapels and double-breasted suits, not like the skinny styles of recent years. Often textured sports jackets. Blue blazers have always been around, but were then more the fashion for WASPS than for Jews, Irish, or Italians. Pants were quite baggy, with pleats and cuffs, unlike the almost skin-tight, cuff-less styles in fashion today. Bell-bottom pants were nowhere to be seen, yet. Ties were thin, or wide, and given to loud patterns of design.

The casual men's clothing of the '50s was more colorful than dress wear. Slacks (otherwise known as pants) were often synthetic, or a mix of wool and rayon, or another polyester. Pleats were uncommon, but the legs still billowed out, narrowing above the ankle. Definitely cuffs below. Slim belts, as a rule, no suspenders. "Walking shorts," solid and plaid, were popular, like Bermuda shorts, just coming down to above the knee. High stockings, sometimes with large diamond patterns, could adorn the lower legs, and not just for Scotsmen or British soldiers.

Shirts outside of dress occasions often were cotton, or mixed with polyester, and had small collars, sometimes button-down. Many were knit like polo shirts now are. Definitely out of style today are the shirt jackets of that era, like many characters wore in *The Sopranos* TV series. These below the waist tunics, by the way, serve to help conceal a growing gut.

When determined to be casual but a bit more dressed-up, a button-up cardigan sweater would do just fine. No pattern, just a monochromatic and singular presentation. Remember Mr. Rogers? Refreshed for us with the 2018 documentary film about him and his "neighborhood" and then Tom Hanks' bioptic portrayal. V-necks were also popular. Casual jackets usually were waist-length, sometimes with a shapely, stretch middle to add to the chest's prominence. Their fabric varied to meet the weather, from cotton to suede and leather. Fedora hats were everywhere in the '50s, sadly not much so in the 21st century. Sports caps, floppy ethnic looking chapeaux, were popular too, and remain common.

Shoes were not a whole lot different from today, except there were more penny-loafers and two-toned saddle shoes. Sneakers were for sports (the best then being *Converse High-Tops*), unlike their ubiquitous presence nowadays as with low and high riders, in colors galore.

Jewelry for men was minimalist in the '50s. No chains, earrings or other body-part piercing, and no wrist bracelets. Wedding and graduation rings and sometimes a colorful stone set in gold or silver were fine. Tattoos were on soldiers (then veterans) and felons.

I probably am not the right person to talk about women's clothing. I have never worn any. My preferences go to simple, tailored styles and muted and solids. Sweat pants, jeans, and a T-shirt, which I like a lot on a woman, were not vogue, as they are today. By the way, no designers, mind you, have, as yet, sought my opinion on these matters.

Here, however, we can record the facts – historical that is, since I don't personally recall what women (middle-class and working women) commonly wore in the 1950s. Except as gloriously portrayed in the Amazon TV series (the first two seasons, the third went astray), *The Marvelous Mrs. Maisel.*

The two styles most worn in women's dress styles were: 1) A thin waisted dress with a shapely bodice that then billowed below, sometimes with a petticoat. The fabric would swing a bit when walking, and more so if a woman was given to twirling. 2) What was called a "pencil" skirt that hugged the thighs and extended a bit below the knees. It was like a sheath. The fabric often was cotton or wool (in winter), sometimes silk; synthetics were emerging, and combined with traditional fabrics, allowed the materials to be lighter, cheaper, and less apt to shrink. A solid color, of any palette, or simple patterns were used; none of the dramatic blocks and shapes and sparkling patterns that followed.

The upper body could have any sort of blouse or sweater. Blouses often were button-down, though there also were knits that molded to the woman's body. Popular with blouses was what was called a "Peter Pan" collar, which lay flat against the blouse, circled the neck, and met in the middle at the front with rounded ends. Sweaters were common, often two-layered (double) cardigans, but not turtlenecks. Stockings often had a seam running down the back and were held up with garters. Women tended to wear cone-shaped, pointed bras, looking almost dangerous to approach. These bras, however, did highlight a thin, tight waist below, like twin peaks set above a small foundation, for those so fortunately endowed.

Capri pants definitely were in style. They were shapely and ended mid-calf. I suppose these were 3-season, not a good idea in 30-degree winter weather throughout most of the country. Shorts went to mid-thigh, no "short-shorts" at the time. Denim was mostly worn by teenagers, then abandoned when a girl became a woman, whatever that means. Swimsuits were mostly one piece, though two-piece suits had entered the scene—but nothing like the bikinis of today.

Women's dress shoes were inclined to have narrow heels, sometimes stiletto, surely as tough to wear back then as now. Flats were also common; they were and still are a lot more comfortable and practical. A preppy approach would be saddle shoes, also called oxfords. These were usually black and white and worn with "bobby socks," white socks rolled down the ankles two or three times.

Outer coats, of wool, or cotton for warmer weather, had a sort of an "A" shape. They grew progressively in width from the shoulders to down below the waist, so they could swing about too. What was it with this capacity for women's clothing to swing about?

Jewelry was a big thing in the '50s, as it was well before that (recall Cleopatra?) – and still is. But I wouldn't dare try to describe its variety of styles, composition, and where on the body it was worn. But I will say that the engagement "rock," the "diamond is a girl's best friend," was what every girl of a middle-class or more prosperous station wanted. I think more so than today, but you can take a look at the ringer-fingers of women you know, in stores, at work, and on the subway, and assess whether it has persisted in popularity.

Why do we put so much stock in clothing? Stare into store windows, internet offerings, print and media clothing ads? Spend money on ourselves, rather than give it to a (more) worthy cause? Regard some styles as out of date, calling for their replacement, even if they still fit?

I used to be a clothing *maven*, liked to dress well, not so much today. Though I try not to look too unkempt, out of touch with proper dressing, what my wife refers to as my looking like a Silicon Valley scientist or entrepreneur. My taste for clothes, and urge to be well-dressed, started with my grandfather, JT. He attired himself well, every workday, and of course at celebrations and funerals. That was his profession if you will; he was a men's haberdasher (I do love that word). The seed was planted early in me, and it did sprout, over time, on its own.

How other people see us, judge us, is a thing. The more uncertain about ourselves we are, the more that matters. Clothes make an impression, in ways good and bad. Best to not look like you have slept in your clothes, borrowed them from someone bigger or smaller, or display a smatter of stains. After those bare essentials, what does how we dress portray? Is there such a phenomenon as "dress for success?" In professional and corporate cultures, in public-facing jobs (like salespeople, teachers, government officials)? In these settings, first impressions count. We want to present ourselves well. Some of our personality, in addition, is conveyed by attire. And there is the showing respect for others, being responsibly attired for a job sought or performed. By caring enough for others to dress properly. What lies below the surface presentation may take some time to demonstrate, and we usually need the chance to get there. In other words, dressing well is way more than being fashionable, which may help in some circles, though ones you might not want to be in.

There is also the inner experience, state of confidence or not, that being dressed well can aid. Self-doubt is about universal among us humans, even if below the surface in those seemingly confident; perhaps more so in those appearing taken with themselves. To doubt is human. So, besides preparation and the support of friends and family, what do we have available to bolster us when seeking opportunity, or at work or in social settings? Other than alcohol, of course. If you guessed clothes—including shoes, especially shoes for some women (and men!)—you get my point.

This aspect of human nature, the wish/need to be well-dressed and thereby demonstrate our station in life and deliver impressions that shape how others see us, has been developed, almost epigenetically engineered, by those who manufacture, market, distribute, and sell clothing. We are their focus and prey. The more clothing counts, the more fashion speaks, the more powerful the impulse to keep buying new stuff, and the more we make the day of clothiers, by augmenting their bank accounts and stock value. There is something to be said about uniforms, for children at school as well as for military personnel, and maybe for uniformity in garments, like wearing Mao-like attire, though not to bow to his or another's authoritarian control.

Consider how much simpler life would be, and already is for those in uniform, if we simply all dressed alike. And modestly so. Imagine what we could do with that money and time. Barack Obama, when he was President, wore the same suit and usually the same shirt and tie every day, except of course for State occasions and on the White House basketball court. Well, not exactly the same suit, but a lot of suits that all looked the same, dark blue in color. He remarked, he has so many decisions to make, why spend any time deciding what to wear?

But unless you are President of the United States, or CEO of Google or Apple (though not Starbucks, where the CEO wears a suit and tie), or in the military, or clergy, or attend a charter school, you likely dress to present the "right" impression, to boost your self-confidence, and incidentally, as well, dignify the role or job you have. Most of us, thus, remain hostage to next year's fashions.

*****

Chapter 8
Orchard Street II

A *Tallis* is a Jewish prayer shawl. It can look like one of those knock-off designer shawls sold on Canal Street, in NYC, only without the parade of colors. It is white, or off-white, with a fringe and elegant, muted stripes. A *Tallis* is to be worn, draped over both shoulders, at prayers in Shul, on Shabbos and the High Holy Days, for daily prayer; even if you are praying at home if you are so inclined. And you need one if you are going to get Bar (or Bat) Mitzvah'd.

Tefillin, also known as phylacteries (which leaves you with no more, perhaps less comprehension of what they are or look like), is a pair of small boxes. They usually come in black and are about the size of a small, jeweler's ring box. They are to be tied (in a way that would challenge an Eagle Scout) around the forehead and arms by orthodox Jews during their prayers. They contain cryptic, parchment messages from the Torah, the Law of God delivered to Moses. Or from the Holy Bible of the Jewish people, the Old Testament—which, by the way, also commands that *Tefillin* be worn as a remembrance of the Exodus when God enabled the Israelites to flee from the evil Pharaoh who had enslaved them. A Jewish youth is expected, as well, to have

Tefillin for a Bar Mitzvah ceremony, though you probably can get away without wearing them, as I did. Just be sure to wear a *Tallis* on the Saturday morning of your passage into "manhood" (for boys of 13 years of age; girls too, like my sister, have a passage, but, their case, not into "manhood").

I didn't know all these rules, in fact hardly any at all, nor lots more about Jewish rituals. These holy accoutrements and orthodox religious practices generally were not practiced by "Reform" Jews; that was a group, closer to the culture of my family, who had moved on to more muted religious and tribal practices, and whose lives were very separate from the orthodox (and ultra-orthodox, like the Hassidim) Jewish communities. My family belonged to what was considered an orthodox Shul, but that was overstating its orthodoxy. My parents went to Shul on Rosh Hashanah and Yom Kippur, the highest of the holy days, once a year, in the fall. We did light Chanukah candles. We were not so acculturated as to have a Christmas tree or wreath.

My Shul was located right off of Boston Post Road, about ¾ of a mile walk from our home. I went there for Hebrew School, after public school two or three times a week—I can't or don't want to remember which. I was 12 and readying myself, through Hebrew learnings, to become a man. The marker to realize was clear: my Bar Mitzvah. But more about that in another story, because this one is about Orchard Street.

Shortly after my 12th birthday (on a Sunday because Saturday is the Hebrew Sabbath and the Lower East Side stores that sold Jewish paraphernalia were shuttered), my father, grandpa JT (my mother's father, an immigrant from

Ukraine), my father and I drove from the Bronx deep into Lower Manhattan, to near Orchard Street, to a shop that sold all things Judaica, including the *Tallis* and those very odd *Tefillin*. JT knew the owner from years frequenting this neighborhood, where he had worked selling fine, but discounted, men's clothing.

I glanced at the store window when we arrived. It looked like a cross between an old book shop and a soon to be demolished antique store. Of course, there was a *Mezuzah* on the door entry, located on the upper right of the wood frame and surely properly blessed.

The *Mezuzah* has Biblical roots: Deuteronomy 6:9, 11:20: "And you shall inscribe them on the doorposts (*mezuzot*) of our house and on your gates." Inside, the simple or ornate small, rectangular, wooden, or metal *Mezuzah* was parchment, with divine instructions to love and obey God (including all His commandments); to believe in only one God; to pass these expectations onto your children. *The Mezuzah* is also a sign to God, so He (She?) would "pass over" your house and thereby provide safety from the unimaginable pain of the taking of the firstborn son—one of the ten deadly plagues the Jewish God visited upon Egypt, well before a more kindly Christ.

I had already begun Hebrew School. I was learning to read and speak the language. To memorize the section of the Torah I would read aloud on the day of my Bar Mitzvah. The Rabbi at my synagogue brooked no questions from his students about what seemed to me to be hard to comprehend about all the mysteries of as well as the judgments and punishments leveled by *Yahweh*, the Jewish Lord. Especially from the likes of me. I was a questioner, a nuisance I guess, which was, with this Rabbi, verboten. His dismissals of my inquiries did not help to make me more of a Jew, though I know now there are many other Rabbis who invite questions and use them to nourish spiritual growth. But not my Rabbi, which made the classes all the more onerous since I mostly wanted to be outside shooting hoops in the playground.

Back to the Judaica shop my grandfather, father, and I had entered, a fitting tile in the mosaic that was the Lower East Side of Manhattan. JT spoke Yiddish to the owner, which my father understood but did not speak. I knew some words and expressions but not enough to keep up with the conversation. I did appreciate that the price needed to be right; we were not there to get the top-shelf, most expensive items. Those were for rich Jews. Plus, my grandfather expected a discount, as a fellow neighborhood worker.

Out came a few prayer shawls, which were made of silk, lustrous and wonderful to touch. The *Tallis* had to be full-sized since it was to last me my lifetime. We picked one, and the owner draped the *Tallis* ceremoniously over my small shoulders. I felt a *frisson*, I guess from the psychic power a religious item can impart on a developing mind. We'll take that one, my father said.

Then we moved to a set of wooden shelves, where small, dark woolen pouches were arrayed, about the size of a small Dopp kit, but not one made by Tumi. They each had a Star of David emblazoned upon them. Inside the pouch were the *Tefillin.* I awkwardly removed the pair of boxes and the long, thin leather bindings that were to affix the boxes to my body. I was then shown how to apply them. The ritual is complicated. It felt way too alien, and I looked even weirder than a 12-year-old already believes he does. But we bought them too. I liked the black bag they came in, with its gold star, like it contained precious jewels, which I guess for some it did. I think I tried putting them on at home once or twice, and never again. My dad had no interest in them, that's for sure. Nor did my grandpa JT. But they did like prayer shawls.

My father paid the shopkeeper, in cash like everything was done back then. I hope he didn't spend very much. JT was very proud of me. My father was relieved the task was done, and quickly lit an unfiltered cigarette once we were on the street. As a reward, not for me but for them, the three of us went to Ratner's, the Kosher dairy restaurant on Delancey Street, a few blocks away. We always ordered blintzes. The Lower East Side was buzzing with people, commerce, outdoor food and garment stands, everywhere.

I wore the *Tallis* when I practiced in the Shul for my Bar Mitzvah. I wore it on the day I became a man, when age 13, which truly was overstating my station in life. I can't remember ever wearing it again. I stuffed the *Tefillin* into the back of a drawer full of socks and shirts since I wasn't going to be looking for them any time soon. I went to synagogue only a few times, for celebrations, like Bar and Bat Mitzvahs, weddings, and much later on dark days after someone close had died and the mourners' *Kaddish* needed saying. I didn't go with my parents when they went on the Hebrew High Holy Days. I was far too restless and what religious faith I had was becoming dissipated, without an institutional anchor, which I had come to steer clear of. The faith and culture of the Hebrews felt too insular to me, as I tried to assimilate in a post-immigrant, second-generational, American way.

Jews, among many other groups, speak of being part of a tribe. A tribe typically separates itself off from the rest of its societal community. It links its members, individuals, and families, with a variety of blood, ethnic, ritualistic, community, and faith-based ties. Often a tribe has its special social, economic, religious and family values, and religious practices; it may speak its own language or a dialect.

I think, nevertheless, that sameness is not a recipe for human growth and development; I tend toward the view that differences are. We can remember that we are all children of Abraham. Yet while we are (presumably) of the same basic roots, one connected family of humankind, diversity is what has spawned over time. We could benefit from seeing diversity as a blessing, a gift that makes us stronger.

The Lower East Side Eastern Europe diaspora Jews of the early 20th century had begun to spread to other NYC boroughs, as well as to Long Island, New Jersey, and Florida – but not Connecticut, yet. Yiddish had been their native tongue, though that was vanishing. But true to the ethnic roots if this "tribe," a hot pastrami sandwich on rye, with Russian dressing, plus a heaping of coleslaw and a big fat pickle, was a form of heaven.

On that day in 1957, as I wandered about what still was the equivalent of a shtetl, alike but different, safer from its counterpart in Eastern Europe, I felt part of the tribe, my tribe. I can't say that feeling has been sustained. I stopped attending Shul, except for celebrations or funerals as I mentioned, never seriously dated a Jewish girl, and all my wives have been Christian. But I feel like a Jew, culturally and ethnically—though not a member of the Jewish faith. Yet, when asked, I say I am a Jew because I am. I still know a fair number of Yiddish words and expressions, and how to pronounce them. Some of my best friends (and many of my family) are Jews.

*****

8A: Jewish People

One often-repeated Jewish joke goes as follows. A Jewish man goes to speak with the Rabbi about the man's son. "Rabbi, I brought him up in the faith, gave him a very expensive Bar Mitzvah and it cost me a fortune to educate him. Then he tells me last week, he's decided to be a Christian. Rabbi, where did I go wrong?"

The rabbi strokes his big, gray beard and says, "Funny you should come to me. I, too, brought up my son as a boy meant to observe the faith, sent him to university and it cost me a fortune and then one day he comes to me and tells me he wants to be a Christian."

"What did you do?" asked the man of the Rabbi.

"I turned to God for the answer," replied the Rabbi.

"What did he say?" asked the man.

He said, "Funny you should come to me." (Referring of course to Christ, the Son of God.)

(Reported by Lawrence Rifkin in the HuffPost, https://www.huffingtonpost.com/lawrence-rifkin/5-best-jewish-jokes-ever_b_7630812.html)

In other words, there are many second and third-generation Jews who leave their religion and tribe. Perhaps more men than women, I don't know for sure—just feels that way. But it seems that we Jewish men today more often find Christian wives (now partners or spouses in the gay community) than did our fathers and grandfathers.

Jews seldom convert to Christianity but tend to become agnostics or atheists, or hold a more general spiritual faith, with no God-head or connection to any religious institution. I am but one illustration. Not many Christians become Jews, either; some women married to Jewish men do since unless the mother is Jewish, the kids are not (unless they convert as adults). On occasion, Christians move from one form of Christianity to another (e.g., from Protestant to Evangelical or Baptist, from Episcopal to Catholic and vice versa, and so forth). Some Christians simply stop going to Church, more so today than in the '50s. But back to me, your narrator: I think of myself as a Jew who has left behind the faith and practice of Judaism. I often wish I had more faith (more about that at the very end of this book).

A long time ago, the Jews declared themselves to be the "Chosen People" or the "Holy People," as described in the Hebrew Bible. The ancient Israelites believed they were chosen because of their special covenant with God. Their religious calling had spread widely by Roman times, in a missionary manner. The light of *Yahweh*, the Jewish God, was to be offered throughout the lands. Their proselytizing did not mean exclusion or discrimination. Non-Jews (*gentiles* or *goyim*, in Yiddish) were not prohibited from living by or benefitting from the spirit, the essence, and practices, of the Jewish faith. Though all men, regardless of their religion, have to wear a *yarmulke* in an orthodox shul. The rabbi teachers of old said this was meant to respect

God's presence, His (Her?) non-exclusive beneficence for everyone. We are, after all, all descendants of Adam and then Abraham, and thus are all His (Her?) creation.

But don't forget, it was the Jews who were "Chosen." You can see how this "special standing" with God might be misunderstood, no less seen as arrogant or in enmity to other faiths and tribes. The Jews multiplied, in ancient Canaan (the Land of Israel), Egypt, Europe, and then were part of a global diaspora. Christ was born a Jew. Persecution has plagued the Israelites from Roman times to the unimaginable Holocaust of the 20th century. Societies need scapegoats, *Painted Birds*, as Jerzy Kosinski wrote, and the Jews (among others) have held that terrible role, awful distinction, since their beginnings.

When I was a boy, seemingly safe in New York City, with all its Jews, including those who held fortunes and power, my family still conveyed a message that only other Jews could be trusted, were the ones who are welcome by marriage to become a part of our family. That was what I faced when I introduced my first serious girlfriend, a Catholic, to my parents. In all fairness, they got over it, but it took a while. We broke up a year later, not because of my family.

A great lesson, teaching device if you will, about the Jews, especially New York Jews, is the *Amazon Prime* TV series, *The Marvelous Mrs. Maisel (TMMM* – especially Seasons 1 & 2*).* Even more so, for me and those of my vintage or lovers of that decade, because the series begins in 1958, a time when I was 13 and hypersensitive to the world around me. Front and center in TMMM are Midge Maisel and her family (the Weissmans, since it is their daughter that is [Mrs.] Maisel), living in an upper west-side, elegant, pre-war building. They are, needless to say, Jewish. The father is a math professor at Columbia, the mother a highly educated stay-at-home mom who raised two kids. We meet their *machatunim*, the in-laws, who are even more *meshuga,* crazier than the Weissmans—in a sweet and generous way; and as a psychiatrist, I think the term "crazy" has to be carefully used. The in-laws own and run a higher-end women's clothing manufacturing factory in the Garment District, well before Donna Karan and far less pricey too. Though they did have gorgeous models, just like the tony brands do today.

As we see in TMMM, with unceasing humor, Jewish families tend not to be quiet, or modest. They are given to forever striving for greater status in their community, and the respect of other members of their respective families or the Shul's Rabbi and congregation, though it does not hurt to have the non-Jews on your side. The kids are spoiled, and expected to stay members of the Jewish tribe, observe the High Holy Days, and continuously demonstrate their capacity to succeed, in business and the professions, especially the men.

The girls, like Midge Weissman (before she married and became Mrs. Maisel), the 20-something daughter (played perfectly by Emmy-winning Rachel Brosnahan, no Jew herself in real life), were to marry, have kids, keep a home, and manage the family's social life. Appearances counted a whole lot, not that they don't today. That was kind of how it was among the Jews back then. Though by the 1960s, my sister included, the lid was beginning to be lifted for Jewish women. The plot in TMMM has Midge, after the collapse of her marriage (divorce was an unspeakable matter back then, almost like cancer), explode into her own, as a woman comic, rare at that time.

Watch TMMM if you want to have an anthropologist's tour of Jews and NYC in the late 1950s. The Catskills too, gentle mountains in Upstate New York, where more prosperous Jews vacationed in the summer, to escape the urban heat, to be entertained, to eat, to eat some more, and for the young women to go husband-hunting. You will be treated to amazing humor. You will witness *tsurus* (heartache) and striving, and the warmth and crazy-making a family creates (though not just Jews). But mostly, you will see the birth, the emergence from her cultural chrysalis, of a young woman, Mrs. Maisel, who does not want it all. She just wants one thing: to be a comic. By the way, you don't have to be Jewish to love this show.

My sister, Marge, faced the quiet suppression of Jewish women. But our mother, Harriet, while generally obeisant to her husband, our dad, worked in the family businesses all her life, and her mother, Rose, every weekday, in rain, winter snow (we had that in NYC regularly then) and summer heat, took the really long subway ride to the Bowery, on the Lower East Side of Manhattan, to work in her brother-in-law's massive antique shop. Women could, should, work, and have a voice, was the implicit message in my family. Bless them. My sister did have to work at achieving her independence, a task all young people face, women and men. She did that very well.

I know that lots of ethnic groups (and the families that constitute them) have their special "color" (character), ways, and complications. In the past 16 years, I have learned a bit about Irish Roman Catholics (RCs), since that is largely my wife's lineage. And she has a big family to teach me. There also were many RCs in my neighborhood as a boy in the northeast Bronx; but back then they were strangers to me, not more than neighbors to say hello to on the street, since mixing among ethnicities didn't happen much. Despite my recent experiences and learning about Irish Catholics, I feel only equipped to speak about the Jews.

I hope you appreciate that my comments, quips too, about the Jewish people come from a pride of membership, and the liberty that allows. Only Jews can get away with making fun of other Jews, without the risk of being seen as anti-Semites.

One high point in my taking considerable liberty with the Jewish people and Yiddish (its most global tribal dialect), was being one of the three authors, in 2013, of a small, 70 pages or so (and not very big in dimensions), blue book called *The Diagnostic Manual of Mishegas*—the *DMOM*! In it, we used Yiddish words, jokes, and anecdotes to parody the American psychiatric diagnostic system of characterizing mental disorders, at the time when the fifth edition of the psychiatric "bible," The *DSM-5* (*The Diagnostic and Statistical Manual*—of mental disorders) was issued. In fact, we beat them to publication date by a few weeks. The *DMOM* divided the human condition into two simple groups, diagnostic categories if you will: *Mishegas* Minor and *Mishegas* Major. Since just about everyone, especially in New York City, is a little *meshuga*, the "Minor" disorder was near to universal, present company included. To have *Mishegas* Major, for example, you have to speak to God—without permission from your Rabbi or insurance company.

And to you, my reader, I say *zie gezundt*. Be well.

*****

Chapter 9
The Road (Block) to My Bar Mitzvah

Rumors are that it is a grand day, a *mitzvah* (a good deed, performed in the service of God), when a boy (or girl) stands at the podium in the prayer room of a Shul on Shabbos. The Rabbi stares over his (or her) shoulder, intent upon the sacred text, as the youth recites a passage from the Torah, in Hebrew, before an assembled group of religious Jewish men and women, and of course family and nowadays a number of Gentiles.

Bar Mitzvah day. Followed by a reception. For those Jews willing to fling money away uselessly (which there were many), there was a big party that evening, with all your friends, relatives, and assorted other unknown attendees who still wanted to give you a big smooch. The party was usually held at a hotel, with a band and lots of food, drink, and dancing.

I didn't think to get Bar Mitzvah'd was such a big deal. That would be going to a Yankee game or someday, maybe, "going all the way" with a girl. However, the rain on the parade leading to my Bar Mitzvah (where I was to become a man, hah!) was that I had to go to Hebrew School. *After* school, two or three times a week, every week. *Except* when there were Jewish holidays, which are ample in number as your Jewish friends can tell you in case you don't know; then you got a bye, but were supposed to go to Shul instead, to pray.

So, about a year before my glorious 13th birthday, I started Hebrew School. As I have emphasized elsewhere (but only if you have been paying attention), I greatly would have preferred to be shooting hoops in the playground, even in the rain. But my parents had paid for the religious preparation, loved the idea of the ritual event (especially my mother), and I began Hebrew School.

I hated it. Not the language, which was interesting, so different in the alphabet, construction, and meaning. You read the written page from right to left, like driving on the "wrong" side of the road in England. I have always liked languages, still do. I seem to have a good ear for pronunciation, so people often think I am better than I am. However, the language notwithstanding, the lessons in history and the Bible, and the stories about the Jewish people, I frequently found preposterous. The Rabbi who was teaching we urchins was not one of the bearded elders. He was still young and dour, without passion for his subjects. Worst of all, he would not brook any questions that implied doubt in the given, the Word, the literalness of the Torah, and the history of the Jewish people. That only made me, contentious as always, ask more questions, thereby stoking more of his disapproval and disdain.

But when it rains, as was happening to me in Hebrew School, think about selling umbrellas. I soon understood.

Being enterprising was what I learned from my father and his friends. They had to go from near poverty to achieve a middle-class life, without more than a high school education. On their own. That meant hustle, drive, and persistence—finding opportunity, seizing it, and not letting go. It had been bred into me over the years.

Meanwhile, how might a kid adapt, even benefit, from his miserable Hebrew school experience? In the North Bronx where I lived, July 4 was a big thing, and it was looming on the horizon when I began Hebrew School. Maybe not as big a deal as in was in Texas or Oklahoma, but we northerners still celebrated. The adults, as a rule, did so by shooting off fireworks. Which were illegal, but readily available, I guess like marijuana and opioids are today. Or booze during Prohibition. I had witnessed displays of fireworks and even had set some off at my uncle's farm in Walden, NY, which he had bought nearby and let my cousin and me have our fun with them, of course under his supervision.

I had seen some kid in my neighborhood, a little older than I, setting off firecrackers. I was mesmerized. I moseyed up to him, watched for a while, and asked, where can I get some?

He said, follow me. We must have walked a mile, and it turned out our destination was close to the Jewish temple, my albatross at the time. We went into an apartment building, took the elevator to the roof, and saw the big sky overhead. We could see other tall buildings and their roofs, features of the North Bronx city-scape. The urban landscape I have come to love.

There were two older boys huddled near one of the low-walled edges of the high roof, the kind that can make you dizzy if you look down from that height. Maybe those boys were even as old as 18! They had brown bags full of stuff, which of course were all forms of firecrackers. They opened some of the brown bags and explained to me this was their stock, their supply of armaments. It was clear these explosive things could make a lot of noise, blow things up, and wow everyone—especially if by surprise. Some were like little bombs, others rockets, and of course the strings of firecrackers that sounded like an automatic rifle (at least the ones I heard on TV). I had a few dollars in my pocket and bought a small assortment, not many since I didn't have much cash for such valuable commodities, even in the 1950s. I secured a small supply, not an abundance. Had I more money, I could have purchased an arsenal.

The next time I duly went to Hebrew School, I hid some of the fireworks in my waist-jacket pocket. Once some of the boys were gathered in front of the Shul before class, I showed them my cache. Wide-eyed, they wanted some! So, I sold them what I had; I am afraid to say, without any safety lecture. I had made a profit! Needless to say, like a pigeon repetitively pressing the reward lever, I soon was back on that roof, buying more supplies, and selling them to my fellow Hebrew School students. Hebrew School was now fun, and lucrative, a reason to go despite the Rabbi and the classes. I can't report this with any pride, at my age today, but back then I was riding high, a small businessman, turning a profit with each exchange. Enterprising, even if a bit shady in my line of work.

Not long after I started this business, my father got a call from the Chief Rabbi of our temple, the one with the long gray beard. My dad was to pick me after Hebrew School and we then were to join the Rabbi in his office. If my father knew why he was summoned, he was not about to tell me. He was not happy, *that* I gathered, about this obligatory, time-consuming, and surely not pleasant, appointment.

We sat down in the Rabbi's book-lined and stuffy office, my dad next to me, both of us in hard chairs. Me facing my doom, I knew. I was not going to be complimented for my good Hebrew accent. The Rabbi said to us that he knew what I had been doing. I said nothing. I realized that someone ratted on me. Then the Rabbi held forth, almost like one of his deadly sermons, instructing me about the danger of firecrackers, the illegality of their sales, and worst of all, the shame of trading in them right in front of the Shul. Holy Ground, I suppose.

I said nothing. What was there to say? I would only be stepping deeper into do-do.

He finally came around to consequences. I remained silent. Maybe I should not be allowed to receive my Bar Mitzvah, the Rabbi remarked, that my offense was that egregious. Silence—now on his part. My father also said nothing, just sat there no doubt devising ways, I imagined, to give me up for adoption. After what seemed like an interminable and insufferable period of time, the Rabbi said, well "maybe" I could continue. This was my first offense if you didn't count being difficult in class (which he also knew about). The temple notices for the Saturday ceremonies ahead had already gone out for the next year (they planned ahead, like trying to get a venue in which to be married in

New York City today). My parents were in deep with deposits and agreed-upon expenses for the Shul reception, the hotel party, tuxedos, the photographer, and, of course, the band. He, the Rabbi, would allow me, for the moment, to continue, to proceed to my Bar Mitzvah. But if I as much as sneezed, I was a goner.

Relief. My father would retain me in the family, for now. And at least I could have the party with my cousins and friends, plus get the famed cash and Treasury Bonds (of small denomination) that came in envelopes from the guests at the celebration, as the evening came to a close. My college fund, I was told, which would help to cover costs even though I surely was going to a basically free, public college—no doubt about that, given the price of private education.

In the car, driving the short distance home, my father said nothing. I had expected him to come down hard on me. But that didn't happen. Nothing happened, including after he surreptitiously told my mother. We had dinner, as usual, there was talk about the business (his business, not mine). My parents had their after-dinner cigarette and I helped my mother clean up, wash, and dry the dishes. We had no "dishwasher"; in my world, at that time, that meant a person or a huge machine in a restaurant.

I knew not to ask my dad about what had happened in the Rabbi's office, my early line of work, and ne'er do well antics. What would be the point? He was not punishing me and, as far as I knew, had no plans to send me to reform school, where I would be beaten to a pulp by far bigger, mean boys. Maybe my father even told his two best friends, Jewish men also making a life with their self-started enterprises—one importing cheap children's clothing and the other owning a jewelry store in Queens. After all, wasn't I following my dad's Semitic, merchant bloodline, creating a (small) business and making a profit?

But I shouldn't have allowed myself to be caught. Looking back, that was my failing.

*****

9A: Enterprise

Like all good Jewish families, mine had made a big deal of my getting Bar Mitzvah'd. My sister too, a few years later, a Bat Mitzvah, though back then there was not the greater parity between the sexes that exists today. Like many first-generation Jewish families, this ritual was vigorously pursued while we simultaneously sought to blend into America, to assimilate, as in to not live in a shtetel. We should aspire to the social status of WASPs, be rich like the Rockefellers, and, of course, be as smart and enterprising as the Jews.

What did I know? We were not a religious family. We were the kind that goes to shul only on the High Holidays and did not keep the Saturday Sabbath, *Shabbos*, as it is known among the Jews, though my mother did change the plates for Passover, and the Passover dinner was always a big deal with too much food and too many relatives. But their firstborn, a son (me), was going to have a Bar Mitzvah, with Saturday morning services at the temple, and a blow-out party that evening, at a fancy hotel in Manhattan (not too fancy, that would break the bank).

The rub, as I mentioned in the story above, was that I had to go to Hebrew School, two (or was it three times) a week *after* school. The *after* was punishment enough because this was not my idea of how to occupy the late afternoons after regular school let out. There was more, as well, to my grievances about going to Hebrew School, though that was not learning the Hebrew language, which I have totally forgotten today (though I still know a little Yiddish from my family). It was the Rabbi and the mindless, literal recitation in classes about "history" and the Bible that were killing me.

Ancient Jewish biblical history is a fable for the most part. But it was taught to me at my Hebrew School as if it were written by God, or those brilliant Rabbis and scholars who actually spoke for him (maybe actually *with* Him—not Her back then) and required the respect due them, exhorted we were. Fables are good, parables too. But literal interpretations of what happened to who, how, when, and for what ostensible moral purpose stretch the imagination, at least mine. There was, however, to be no questioning the word of God, and, of course, his Bronx rabbinical emissaries in 1957 and 1958, the years of my training to become a man in the Jewish tradition.

When I dared to ask a question—or several—of the Rabbi who taught our class, to try to find some shred of logic between story and reality, I got the most awful scowl. After doing that a few times, I was kept after "after" school, killing any possibility of getting to a basketball court. I was told I should not question. I thought, however, that it was in the Jewish DNA to question. Remember, even for non-Jews, the *Four Questions* asked at the Passover Seder? I admit I was rather persistent in my questioning, egged on no doubt by the Rabbi becoming annoyed with my Hebrew School educational inquiries. By the way, I did not reserve my difficult self for the Shul; I was no different at home with my mother and other relatives, though sparingly with my father, who usually made it clear he was in no mood for being bothered.

We will return presently to my Hebrew School experience and the near catastrophe of not being allowed to go to the Altar to read, and thus foreclosed from manhood. And what it meant to my father and mother.

But first, let's have some more context—what was happening in New York, the US, the world, in the year when I was to be Bar Mitzvah'd? 1958.

Dwight Eisenhower, "Ike," was in his second term as President. He would sign legislation to create NASA (The National Aeronautics and Space Administration), in response to the launch of the Soviet satellite, Sputnik, which had been sent skyward and blanketed the news. But the Soviet glory would be eclipsed by "Explorer 1," the United States' first satellite rocket launched from Cape Canaveral, Florida. For a nerd like me, this was magical stuff. The following year, I would go to The Bronx High School of Science, where real scientists are bred, not just doctors and lawyers.

The microchip was co-invented at Texas Instruments and Robert Noyce of Fairchild Semiconductors; it was subsequently further refined and marketed in the US by Intel. I knew about semiconductors because my father invested in Texas Instruments, and did well in that purchase. Maybe it helped finance the Bar Mitzvah?

Robert F. Wagner Jr. was in the first of his three terms as Mayor of New York City. W. Averell Harriman, a Democrat, was finishing his one term as Governor of the state, to be succeeded by Nelson Rockefeller, a Republican whose legacy he then built over three terms in Albany. The city and the state were under the grip of a deep recession in 1958, which brought unemployment to 7%. But my family and its stationery store business were doing fine, buying big cars, like Oldsmobiles, one of Detroit's finest (but not quite a Cadillac).

The Yankees won the World Series, yet again, in the seventh game, beating the Milwaukee Braves. I did live in the Bronx, though not near the stadium. The "Bronx Bombers" had created glee and pandemonium—all about the City.

American music was at an apogee: we had Elvis, Johnny Cash, Buddy Holly, Little Richard (*Good Golly Miss Molly*), The Platters, The Everly Brothers (*Wake Up, Little Susie*), Jerry Lee Lewis (*Great Balls of Fire*), Connie Francis (*Who's Sorry Now*), The Silhouettes (*Get A Job*), and even the Kingston Trio. A song that continues to irritate to this day, in its saccharine way, *Volare*, was the number one single of the year.

In Vietnam, there were growing uprisings by the Viet Cong against the South Vietnamese government. My family often watched the evening news (*CBS News*, then hosted by Douglas Edwards, who preceded the legendary Walter Cronkite). I wondered where in the world was this jungle? It would be some years before the US was snagged into this war – our entry born of paranoia about Communism. The war's continued prosecution would—over a decade later—

lead to me being drafted, as a young doctor in residency training. That's another story.

I was drawn to libraries, basically to borrow science and science fiction books. But there was talk among those more erudite than me about Boris Pasternak (1890-1960), the Russian novelist and poet who had won the Nobel Prize in literature. He had given us *Doctor Zhivago*, the story of a love-torn Russian medical officer stationed in a small village. The plot was set against the frozen tundra, to add to its suffering and bleakness. Zhivago is married, with his wife and son living in Moscow, when he meets Lara, herself married but her soldier husband is missing. Zhivago happens upon Lara a second time, as he is foraging for food and firewood for his now destitute family. The drama heightens as he is captured by the opposing army, during a civil war, where he is forced into labor as a doctor. Upon release, he resumes his affair with Lara, but it is short-lived, and circumstances take them their separate and tragic ways.

There is more to this marvelously drawn tale, of course. But the tragedy of it all—romance, war, separations of lovers and their children, psychic and physical suffering, forced labor and relationships—was a metaphor for its Russian era and the insistent, unmet longings of we humans. The grandness of plot, the elegant story-telling: *The Great War* (WWI), the October Red revolution, and of misery momentarily mitigated by love, were glorious Nobel material. But, as I recall, when starting the book while standing in the stacks of the NY Public Library on 42nd Street, it was far too thick a volume for me, in more ways than one. The film version was released in 1965 when I was old enough to absorb the story and some of the metaphors of *Dr. Zhivago*. The movie was a staggering 3 hours and 17 minutes long, directed by David Lean; it starred Omar Sharif, Julie Christie, Alec Guinness, Geraldine Chaplin, and Rod Steiger. It was a blockbuster.

The Nobel Peace Prize was awarded to Georges Pire, a stranger to my insular life. He was a Belgian priest, renowned for his work as an army chaplain in WWII, during the resistance to German occupation, and later for his humanitarian work with European refugees. My family was too insular to know about him or his recognition, though we always had stories of the holocaust, meant to imply that Jews could truly trust no one except members of our own religion. But Pire's life, and others like him, were what I came to admire once I left my family in the Bronx, and began school at the restive City College of New York.

Yet, in 1958, as I approached my thirteenth birthday, my life proceeded in its seriously limited manner. I was busy at school, public and religious, and in playgrounds when the time allowed. I was a better student, thinker, than an athlete, for sure. Which brings us back to the trouble I had in Hebrew School.

I had made a connection in the Bronx to buy firecrackers. It was spring and July not far away. All very clandestine, and illegal. I could go to a nearby apartment building as described in the story above, at appointed hours, take the elevator to the roof, and choose among a variety of fireworks. The "dealers" were kids older than me, but probably still in high school. I don't think they were Jewish. The supply, from which I could choose, included packs of firecrackers, 20 in a chain; cherry bombs (known to blow up a toilet bowl, I was told, if so inclined); fiery Roman

Candles; Ground Spinners; Sparklers, as well, for the very tame. I had some money, and for me, that meant an opportunity to buy and sell. I was, as it turned out, an enterprising young man.

And at the Hebrew School, I had customers! Boys my age who were eager to buy, who had some pocket money and wanted to blow things up.

So, I started my own, low-overhead, high-margin firecracker business. This seemed as natural to me as it must have been to my father, who was a businessman, though he sold stuff that was legal. Business was in my family's blood. Purchasing and selling merchandise was how my family had made its living, pursuing the American dream, for several generations. Now, I too was running a business. Though, of course, I couldn't share the pride in my enterprising ways with my parents.

Then one of the boys ratted on me. No doubt seeking the Rabbi's praise and goodwill.

I only had a clue I was caught when my father was called by the head Rabbi and told he was come to the school to meet with me and the Rabbi. Of course, at a time of day when he would have had to leave his own business early to deal with his errant son.

We dutifully arrived at the temple and sat outside the Rabbi's office. I knew I was in big trouble: I was selling illegal and dangerous items, not in the shul, but in its holy shadow, or something like that. He questioned whether I could proceed with my Bar Mitzvah, given my conduct.

Oy, I thought. Not that I cared, but I knew how big a deal it was to my parents, grandparents, and other enmeshed family members. But I was to be given a second chance, merciful as was the Rabbi, and the Temple, which after all had booked that morning, and taken down-payment money for the ceremony, education, and likely, as well, a requisite, handsome donation to Israel, or the new wing of the Temple.

No more selling firecrackers. No more being the pain in the ass I was in class. Plus, perfection in my language skills and Torah reading. Those were the terms, and they surely were not negotiable. I sat there like a stone, and my father agreed. Though, I recall noticing that my father had a twinkle in his eye, not watering like his eyes did sometimes from chain-smoking Camels. A twinkle was not what my father customarily demonstrated, except sometimes with his men friends. Turns out, he was proud of me that day, in his own way. I was not the hopeless, lazy youth he imagined but an enterprising young man, following in the family's merchant tradition. I was even selling goods used to celebrate America, the land of opportunity, especially in the 1950s.

His mind was well beyond the scolding I got from the Rabbi. He seemed to see me in a new way; he could take secret pride in his son. Go figure. I now was a young businessman. That was what he must have concluded from my misdeeds. He told my mother what had happened, and shut down any conversation about concerns she might have had. The Bar Mitzvah was still on, which was what really counted to her. There was never another word said about the firecrackers.

I sensed, however, that my passage into being a man had begun, *not from* the Jewish Temple *but at it*, where I had started a business. Fortunately, no one was injured, and my profits, such as they had been, were not confiscated by my parents.

The quality and capability I evidently had shown was that I was enterprising. I was a kid who saw opportunity, stuffed it into a paper bag to peddle, and was running a profit-making business. Being true to the ethos of my family, especially that of my Depression-era old man. Being enterprising was *a mitzvah*, a good deed (in Yiddish) and among the Yids. I had displayed the markings of being both a good Jewish merchant *and* a prideful American.

It was like a moment of opportunity in our "land of opportunity" that I had seen and grasped. Until I got caught—but only because some other boy, surely envious, wanted to do me in. I don't think it was to replace me in business, a "hostile takeover," since my customers then went unserved, which did not make them happy. That rat got the better of me, and that, I realize, is one danger of doing well—making money, being at the head of my class, even if it was not in Hebrew School.

*****

PS: I refrained from any more munitions dealing at the temple, which was my only site of business. Too risky to try it at public school; too many there to rat on me. I did my job ably reading the Torah on a sunny Saturday in May of 1958, and kosher wine and food was served in the temple. That night, I dressed in a tuxedo with a fresh haircut. We had a big party, with an orchestra, lots of dancing, and some girls my age—not to mention my family. The envelopes of *gelt* (money) duly came my way at the end of the evening. It was rather like yet another business, though this one financed by my family and in no violation of the law, American or Hebraic. That money, however, would be stowed away in Treasury Bills (remember those?) for my future education. I had made it through that thicket of trouble and had a cool notch on my belt. I can't recall the next time I went back to Shul.

Chapter 10
Stayin' Alive

I went to junior high—now known as intermediate or middle school (what was it about "junior" that led to its demise?) at P.S. 113 on Barnes Avenue in the Bronx. I was one of the true nerds, as evidenced by my having passed a "special school" entrance test in the sixth grade. Not that I had any idea I was even taking the test, no less a qualifying exam. But I was to be admitted to the SPs (Special Progress class). I would be able to speed my way through the three years of junior high school in two, with some 25 other off-center kids, boys, and girls. I was about the youngest member of the sixth-grade class so I would be ensuring, likely augmenting and accelerating, my massive insecurity and 11-year-old maladroitness. I still wonder why the program was called the SPs as if we had some developmental problems that required "special" attention.

In the SPs, I met Raymond Eisenstark, whose mental capacities surely put my myopic view that I must have been kind of smart into perspective. For example, the math teacher would give the class a complex calculus problem, which I would begin to labor and suffer with. But at a nearby desk, in seconds, it felt like even less, Raymond would have it done. And done right, not a hasty piece of sloppy brain work, but perfect and really fast. Once in a while, I would beg him for a clue. I felt like a disgrace, a kid who did not warrant the invitation to this school for smart kids. Maybe my invitation to the SPs was a mistake? After all, I was no shining star orbiting in the same universe as Raymond. The same troubling problem happened in physics, where I performed better (for me) but Raymond still was in another league. I learned then what *really* smart was—a personally humbling experience that carries a big punch, you know what I mean?

Early in my second (and final) year at 113, at the ripe age of 12, I and the other SP kids (and maybe some others) took the city-wide exam for New York City's handful of special entrance schools, like Stuyvesant, Music and Art, and Bronx Science. Another test I don't recall taking.

Sometime later, I received a letter (remember those?) congratulating me on my acceptance into Science. I showed the letter to my parents. I said I didn't want to go there. My friends were going to Evander Childs, on Gun Hill Road, where some of the kids wore leather jackets. I wanted to go there, with them. Totally unlike them, especially my mother, my parents said nothing. That was shrewd since at that age, fighting me would about guarantee I would decline Science and go to Evander. A week or so later, I thought I would be less bored at Science. Plus, my school friends were not exactly like my cousins in Queens, whom I loved and spent endless hours with. Besides, I didn't have a leather jacket and knew my parents would never buy me one. So, I went to Science.

We lived in the Northeast Bronx, near where Eastchester Road almost touched Gun Hill Road, which was where the old IRT subway station could be found. Our neighbors were mostly first-generation, (lower) middle-class Italians, Irish, and Jews. To get to Science from our attached, three-decker, red-brick home, I had to take two buses, which took a fair amount of time, then walk near to half a mile to the school. Which was fine since I didn't exactly have a busy calendar or need an assistant to manage it. The new Bronx Science building, on West 205th St., opened the year I began. It was impressive—modern and unlike the old, beat up, New York City public schools I had come to know. Now I was really among kids who were apt to be pariahs because they were so smart. We were a community of able, industrious, and over-achieving kids.

But there was one problem. And it wasn't within the walls of the school. Nor was it academic.

The "new" Bronx Science had been built next to a legendary New York, also public, all-boys high school where entrance seemed determined by the size of a kid's neck or his zeal in tormenting other (smaller) boys. DeWitt Clinton. Clinton had the best high school football team in the City, I recall. Science did not have a football team.

The other sport the Clinton boys excelled at was identifying and harassing Science students, boys only it seemed, who usually arrived by the same buses or walked there on the same, open and wide blocks leaving no place to hide. Especially dangerous was school dismissal time since the Clinton kids seemed to have been operating some sort of surveillance system; they were like on patrol, watching for those boys who left the Science building, and then beelined in small groups to taunt us. Kids like me were especially at risk because we had normal (or small) size necks, wore glasses, and could not readily conceal the stack of thick books we carried (before backpacks!). We also had no cleats hanging on our shoulders.

The Science book store sold slender, acetate-coated book covers that proudly displayed the school logo. I thought they were very cool. I bought a few. Then it dawned on me that using them to adorn my textbooks would be like ferrying fresh meat among starving wolves. So, I carried as few books as I could, left the Science covers at home, and plotted out my daily escape from the planet of the apes. Only a few times was I surrounded and taunted, but never took a blow. I don't know why, maybe not reacting too much from being in a state of total body paralysis, or being zoned-out, distracted, and distant with thoughts about how my parents would take the news of my death from a call by the school Principal, maybe Vice-Principal since they tended to have to do the dirty work. Perhaps I was too small a prey, the kind of fish you have to throw back in because of size limits? My daily mission, for those three long years, was *stayin' alive*.

You might think living in New York City was a dangerous place to be. But not so, not in the Bronx in the mid-1950s. Even the South Bronx, which would gain infamy in years to come, "Fort Apache," was OK, at least before dark. You also had to stay away from where drugs were dealt and used, which was not hard to determine because of how collapsed and desperate the neighborhood would appear. A similar geographic evasion also was needed when I started in college, in Harlem, at The City

College of New York (CCNY). I had to get off the 145th Street subway station and walk south, because the 125th Street station, and 125th Street itself, was not a place a white kid should be.

While I experienced the terror of the Dewitt Clinton boys because I was a Science student, I don't have any recall of anti-Semitism in my neighborhood or schools. But that may have been because I was indeed quite segregated from the general population of neighborhood youth and students when I was both in junior high and high school.

There also were almost no blacks or Hispanics in those schools, a disparity that needed fixing and would *begin* to be remedied soon thereafter. But still not enough, even today. There still are SPs classes in NYC, with transparent admission standards. Science (and Stuyvesant), just to name a couple of public exam schools in NYC, continue to have an aura emanating from their competitive admissions process, academic excellence, the caliber of students (and teachers), and the career successes of their graduates.

When I went to my 25th Science reunion at the school (well over 25 years ago, more about Science reunions in a later chapter), I noticed the demographics of the then-current student body had changed, as did the award plaques on the walls: Instead of a lot of Jews, Asians had come to dominate the population, especially the top students. And because now I live near (the new but no longer actually new) Stuyvesant, I see today the flood of kids arriving and leaving, and they too are significantly Asian, with some who are black and Hispanic. Bless the progress, though not yet enough, of equity and opportunity for New York's rainbow of people.

City College, by the way, upended its entrance policy (about four years after I graduated) to what was termed "open admissions": No superior school grades or strong aptitude exam performance were required. That was good and bad. Good because it gave an educational opportunity to many youths of color, who often suffered the consequences of the poor-quality education in their neighborhoods. That had, thus, left many behind in reading, math, science, and critical thinking. Bad because the overall academic excellence of the school diminished, and quite a few great teachers decided to leave, or never joined the faculty. This open-admissions policy was never overtly changed, though it was creatively side-stepped by establishing "special" schools within the College, where the high achievers could go.

Stayin' alive was one of the useful things I learned at Bronx Science. I am still here, haven't been mugged yet. Bronx Science was good preparation, in more ways than I had imagined, for the rest of my life.

*****

10A: Living in Safety

Bullies have darkened many a school climate. Bullies are scared people posing as conquerors. They strike out to conceal their weaknesses. Not that understanding this dynamic excuses their behavior, which has become anathema in most school settings. But understanding what drives bullying behavior points to how its genesis might be prevented. When carefully excavating the personal histories of bullies, we learn that the great predominance of them were victimized themselves, by parents or other relatives. Sandor Ferenczi, an early Eastern European psychoanalyst, called the phenomenon by which victims become perpetrators as an "identification with the aggressor." "The Stockholm Syndrome" is a more modern version of this counter-intuitive behavior.

It is not only schools and neighborhoods that want for safety. Families tragically can be sites of domestic violence, neglect and abuse, active substance dependence, including alcohol, opioids—pills and heroin (and now Fentanyl)—as well as crack cocaine and crystal meth. Home also may be where instability reigns as a result of untreated serious mental illness (like the psychotic states of schizophrenia and bipolar disorder). Housing, as well, can be unsafe—with violence in the lobby, doorway, or elevator, often the by-product of black-market drug dealing or gangs. Or more insidiously, danger in housing can be from building lead or asbestos, ambient diesel fumes, and even mold.

We also now face what has been called "the new normal," namely the unpredictable eruption of terrorist acts. These have been perpetrated, more recently, by trucks and home-made bombs since hijacking an airplane for use as a weapon has become almost impossible (the 1997 film, *Air Force One,* with Harrison Ford, Gary Oldman and Glenn Close, notwithstanding). Terrorist acts maim, kill, and heartlessly eviscerate the souls of families and survivors. They are meant to not only execute bodily violence, they aim also to destabilize a community and hurt an economy.

Violence against civilians to advance political or ideological goals is ultimately unstoppable (in its entirety)

147

because it's so varied means – like guns, pipe bombs, packages loaded with poison, and vehicles – are everywhere and accessible. We are learning and messaging that vigilance, especially by all of us in our respective communities—not only technical surveillance, "eyes in the sky"—has and will save a lot of lives. To tolerate the "new normal," we have slowly become reconciled to the existence of random terror, to "there but the Grace of God go I." American society is now living with this reality, which is far greater in New York and Boston than smaller, less visible cities across the country; I think this calls for protections commensurate with risk, but I live in NYC. European nations, the UK and Asia also live with the horrific specter of when and where the next attack will strike, as terrorist cells propagate well beyond the Middle East. I wish I could imagine an end in sight, but that would be a vision clouded by the cataracts of denial.

There are, of course, also hate crimes. I think mass murders by solo, younger men with their high-powered, automatic rifles are hate-driven, meant to satisfy a burning rage or revenge, a felt injustice, and deliver a moment of recognition, "glory", in a life without any distinction or contribution. In the US, a mass murder (defined by four or more people seriously injured or killed) happens on the average of every day. Over 300 a year. What is it in this country that rifles designed for military action are so readily accessible to those deranged enough to use them, on strangers?

Hate crimes, profane attacks, and murders, also may be directed at an ethnic, racial, or religious group. These now happen at liberal political gatherings (infiltrated by "alt-right" extremists and neo-fascist thugs), and where gays and trans people congregate, to name a few examples. African-Americans have lived under the threat of hate and assault since the beginnings of the United States, with no abatement after American slaves were "liberated." Police brutality in cities large and small, not just southern, seems a newer and sustained form of black oppression, as is the injustice of the American courts and penal systems, which profoundly disadvantage people of color. What an abyss we have fallen into.

In other words, violence in our society is ubiquitous. Everyone is a potential victim, though being white and privileged significantly reduces the odds.

Violence seems to me to be different from aggression. Aggression is a basic human drive, a human characteristic, in the same category as hunger, sex, and attachment. Violence, apart from war and self-protection, instead, has a gratuitous quality, it need not be. It is aggression gone awry. Violence is not a means of survival, as can be aggression and our other drives.

Geoffrey Canada's (the renowned educator, especially for his creation of the *Harlem Children's Zone*) first book was titled *Fist Stick Knife Gun: A Personal History of Violence* (2010). Drawing upon his life growing up in the South Bronx, Canada told the story of his family, neighborhood, and of the progression in weapons used in street fights. First, it was fists, then sticks, then far more damaging and deadly weapons like knives, and finally guns, the fearsome "equalizer." Guns have ushered in a new, horrific level of violence on the streets, as well as in homes. The victims of most gun fatalities are a close relative of the perpetrator, not a stranger breaking into a home. Canada, as a boy, personally witnessed this progression in the weapons used in his neighborhood. But he had the good fortune of having a strong family, coupled with his own grit, faith, and intelligence. He escaped alive—and went on to thrive. Not that many do. Canada's work as an adult, fashioned by his experiences and learning, has sought to enable other inner-city poor youth exposed to the dangers of their local streets to find ways to elude the looming dangers. The tools he offers are education and support, and a vision of a different and better life.

Many youths, however, are not raised in tough, merciless neighborhoods. Yet, while a middle-class, middle-American existence may help to reduce the gravity of exposure to unsafe communities, homes, and families, it is no guarantee. By far.

1998 saw the groundbreaking scientific publication in the American Journal of Preventive Medicine, by Vincent Felitti and Robert Anda, of a study of 17,337 adult volunteers, with an average age of 57 (The Relationship of Adult Health Status to Childhood Abuse and Household Dysfunction, *American Journal of Preventive Medicine,* 1998, Volume 14, pages 245–258). About half were women, three quarters were white, and the same percentage had attended college. The study's participants were all members of the Kaiser Health Maintenance Organization (HMO), in San Diego, California. In other words, this was not about inner-city poor people, where trauma and adversity too often flourish. This report put us all on notice that childhood is rife with insecurity, suffused with the danger of trauma during our developmental years.

This large group survey was conducted in collaboration with The Centers for Disease Control and Prevention (CDC), during the years 1995–1997. Study participants completed a confidential questionnaire that asked about whether they had experienced childhood maltreatment and family dysfunction. Their health at the time also was assessed, including a physical exam and recording details of their health status and lifestyle behaviors. This information was combined and sorted to become the collective data of the study. All participants were asked about whether they had experienced any of a number of different forms of childhood trauma, before the age of 18. The researchers termed that exposure as Adverse Childhood Experiences (ACEs). ACEs included emotional, physical, and sexual abuse; emotional and physical neglect; homes with active domestic violence, or untreated drug, alcohol, or serious mental disorders; those homes where there had been parental separation or divorce; or having a family member who was incarcerated.

What was so groundbreaking about this study was its ability to link, substantively (though by correlation not direct causation), ACEs with later life physical and mental problems. It revealed how childhood trauma was instrumental in producing enduring suffering. The World Health Organization (WHO) incorporated the ACE Study questionnaire in its report on *Preventing Child Maltreatment: A Guide to Taking Action and Generating Evidence* (October 2006).

Trauma, we have observed from incessant media coverage, is not only inflicted by families, or neighborhoods. It can be delivered at the hand of teachers, coaches, clergy, doctors, film and TV producers, and from too many other fronts, by those who have power over our lives or careers.

We have discovered that ACEs are additive in their impact. An early life that accumulates 4 or 5 ACEs, or more, is a powerful predictor of illness and despair, often by adolescence. The later consequences of ACEs on affected youth include alcohol and drug abuse; depression; heart, lung, and liver diseases; STDs (sexually transmitted diseases); intimate partner violence; smoking, especially at an early age; suicide attempts; and unintended pregnancies (children having children). As the number of ACEs a youth experiences increase, so too does their risk for multiple physical and psychic morbidities.

ACEs appear to wreak their damages in two principal ways: First, by inducing a chronic stress response in the brain, which is expressed in our bodies, particularly by hyperactivity of the adrenal glands. The adrenals, little but powerful glands that sit atop our kidneys, are signaled to release a sustained flood of cortisol (the stress hormone). Excess body cortisol lowers immunity to host of diseases (from colds to cancer), as well as our capacity to recover from them (resilience).

Secondly, chronic stress induces a persistent inflammatory response in our body, which lays down those nasty, fatty plaques in cardiac and cerebral arteries, putting us at greater risk for heart attack and stroke. Chronic inflammation attacks pancreatic cells, where it can breed diabetes. It also destroys skeletal joints, where osteoarthritis is hastened and worsened. Chronic inflammation, we now also know, is a critical driver in the development of a variety of mental illnesses, including depression, addiction, PTSD, even schizophrenia. Alzheimer's, too, is associated with chronic inflammation in the brain.

As if that were not enough, traumatic childhood events are highly associated with behavioral (habit) disorders, like smoking cigarettes (or today delivering nicotine to the brain by vaping tobacco), alcohol and drug dependence, and unprotected sex (which increases exposure to HIV/AIDS and genital herpes, not to mention unwanted pregnancy).

As I have written before, "Chronic stress and inflammation are the enemy." Fueled by adversity and trauma (quantifiable by an ACEs questionnaire, in childhood and adulthood), disease and disorder mount and limit functioning and quality of life, as well as usher in disability and early death (*Shonkoff JP, Garner AS, Siegel BS, Dobbins MI, Earls MF, Garner AS, McGuinn L, Pascoe J, Wood DL. The Lifelong Effects of Early Childhood Adversity and Toxic Stress. Pediatrics. 2012 Jan;129(1):e232-e246. Epub 2011 Dec 26. PubMed PMID: 22201156; Association of Childhood Adversities and Early-Onset Mental Disorders With Adult-Onset Chronic Physical Conditions: Scott, KM, Korff, M, ScD; Angermeyer, MC Benjet, C, Bruffaerts, R, de Girolamo, G, Haro, JM, Le'pine, J-P, Ormel, J, Posada-Villa, J, Tachimori, H, Kessler, RC, Archives of General Psychiatry Volume 68, August 2011*).

The field of public health, where I have spent the past two decades, helps us appreciate both the risk and protective forces at work that shape the experience of safety – in both children and adults. When communities and families can reduce the risks of trauma, and when they better foster its protective factors, the calculus of harm and benefit is changed, with lives spared and their quality enhanced.

No discussion of safety is complete without considering human attachment. The two principal styles of attachment described in my field are called "secure" and "insecure"; each can be recognized as early as at one year of age. Both, in their powerful ways, will determine differently how a child responds to the challenges of development; these include the capacity to be alone, to act with some confidence of self-expression and in relationships, as well as in the capacity for intimacy with others. If secure attachment is not attained in early childhood, its troubled legacy continues into adulthood.

Secure attachments, in adults, are evident when a person can put into perspective the inescapable disappointments, frustrations, separations, and minor traumas of being alive. People with secure attachments are more resilient to life's slings and arrows. They can be emotionally close to others, to receive and provide intimacy, and allow themselves to depend upon others while being responsibly dependable themselves.

Insecure attachments appear in three principal ways, though more than one may co-exist in any individual.

Dismissive/avoidant personality types tend to distance themselves from others. They don't seem to place significant value on relationships. Some may show a type of faux independence, which can make them appear strong, at least on the surface. When reliable information about their early lives can be obtained, there often is evidence of parental neglect or outright rejection.

Preoccupied/anxious types are highly focused on their relationships. They puzzle as to whether they can depend on others, as well as how others may see them (and thus treat them). These highly worried individuals tend to remain connected to and reliant on parents or others who served in caregiving roles in their lives, however limited or flawed. They also can behave as emotionally starved, desperate for connection, which disposes them to acting in dependent, child-like ways.

Disorganized types have the greatest problems with adult relationships. They can be interpersonally dramatic and unstable. Many with this form of insecure attachment suffered early trauma by abuse or neglect, or the loss of a parent, or lived in a home or housing wanting for physical safety (as also seen in war-ravaged cities and in forced refugees). Their deep insecurity can lead to intense, abortive relationships, even at times to desperate, self-destructive efforts to maintain a connection.

Pronounced attachment problems tend to become multi-generational, as the insecure child later becomes the troubled mother (or father) to the next generation's children.

Considering these vagaries, vulnerabilities, and complexities of our early lives and environments, it seems a miracle to emerge somewhat intact. Yet it happens, all the time. The odds are improved, however, when communities function, when families are taught the skills to better parent and communicate with each other and their children, when educational opportunities are accessible, where work delivers a living wage, and when hope for a better future is kept alive.

*****

Chapter 11
A Safe Place to Be Smart

Mentioning the Bronx (the New York City borough that sits atop Manhattan, for those who may not know this city) can conjure up *Fort Apache the Bronx*, the film from 1981, with Paul Newman and Danny Aiello. The movie portrayed the danger and desperation that then boiled in sections of the Bronx, especially the South Bronx.

I grew up in the Bronx, named after a Dutchman (Jonas Bronck) when the city was settled centuries ago. First, New York City was called New Amsterdam, but that didn't last long.

Indeed, there are still some pretty sketchy places in the Bronx, though gentrification has consumed a lot of the borough. But there was another form of danger—one among some boys, usually big or in packs, that made it frightening to be smart, wear (thick) glasses or tote a lot of books coming or going from school. My junior high school in the North Bronx, P.S. 113, was a little like that. I had to avoid other, bigger, mean boys who were looking to bully and shame, in the hallways, locker room, and gym. But because I was segregated, if you will, for two years in the Special Progress class with the same group of other nerdy kids, boys, and girls, we were mostly sheltered from the storm about us.

There was then, still is today, a New York public school, citywide exam for ninth graders that any city resident youth can take. Of course, kids (and their families) living in under-resourced neighborhoods could have no idea about the exam and were not generally educated well enough to succeed, which is needed beyond what native intelligence may contribute. These are youth who need a larger vocabulary, as well as reading and writing skills, math, and science to stand a chance at gaining entrance. It makes a big (bad) difference, as well, if these young people experienced food insecurity at home (not knowing if food would be on the table) or housing instability (not knowing if they would be able to continue to live in the same home, or even in a nearby neighborhood). Not fair, of course. We have so much more to do to achieve equity.

The ninth grade in my time was the last year of "junior high" (seventh through ninth grade—the educational waystation between elementary and high school). To my surprise, as I neared the end of ninth grade, I received notice that I had been accepted into the Bronx High School of Science. A public school, with no tuition. Me and about 900 other teenage New Yorkers, from throughout the city.

"Science" was one of several "exam schools" (like Stuyvesant and The High School of Music and Art) where smart and talented city kids could go for free – unlike private schools, and with no quotas to exclude Jews, blacks, Hispanics, or Asians. It was a school whose entrance was determined by merit, meaning intelligence, decent preparatory public education, and surely a good dose of industriousness. Science was a school that academically rivaled the private schools that served the rich and privileged—not including the (also private) Catholic Schools, and there have been some very fine ones in the City.

There was great inherent bias in the city's special schools' entrance exam, since growing up in poverty, violence, or hunger did not foster achieving good scores on standardized examinations. But fortunately for me, those had not been my circumstances. Somehow, on the exam, I had made the cut and was to be a student at the stellar Bronx High School of Science. Sometimes, I thought the admissions office must have confused me with someone with a similar name, like Federer (the fabulous tennis player, but that was well before his time and fame). But, come to think of it, I also had gained entrance to the junior high school SPs, doing three years in two. Maybe, at least, I knew how to score well on public school entrance exams.

My first reaction to getting into Science was that I didn't want to go. My junior high friends were not accepted; they were going to the local high school. That's what I said to my parents, who—remarkably—did not fight me, letting me come around to accepting admission. That was 1959, when Italians, Irish, Jews, and a few other "minorities" chiefly inhabited the Bronx and Northern Manhattan. The vast diaspora of American immigrants (these and many national and ethnic groups) was trying to succeed in a more just society, which had been foreclosed to them in their homelands because of religion, class, color, economic, or social standing. Education was the means to get ahead when I was young, maybe not quite as much as wealth but pretty good. And Bronx Science was the in the Ivy League of public high schools, and not just in NYC.

Some years ago, I attended my 50th (!) Science reunion. Badges showed our photos from the graduation yearbook since these were the images that formed an emotional memory, deep in the brain's hippocampus, for recognizing one another. Some 200 alumni, spouses, and friends crowded into a Chelsea, New York, restaurant for an evening of immersion in memories as well as collectively considering today's realities. Drink in hand, I tried to brave walking into the crowd. "Start a conversation with someone, anyone," my wife said when I froze. So I did. There were only a handful of people I knew, but there were so many others who had been my classmates, vintage New Yorkers every one of them, no matter where they lived today.

Reunions tend to eliminate two groups, not including those whose schedule simply will not permit attendance: Those who do not want to put their lives on display and those who are sick, housebound, or who have died. A third group, those who did not want to attend, are more of a mystery to me—take me, for example, since I had only attended one other reunion (the 25th). Maybe a remnant of the social insecurity I felt so much as a youth, not that my confidence or conviviality is so good today.

The master of ceremonies for our 50th began the evening with a morbid reading of the names of 71 "Class of '62" graduates who had died. They were listed "In Memoriam" in the program. I could have done without the reading. There were only a few of the deceased I knew personally, but the sheer number of those who had passed as well as the homage paid to them by friends who commented during the recitation was a reminder of how thin is the thread of life, as we know it. It was like starting the evening with taps.

One fellow I knew well when we both were young had died over a decade ago. We were in the same junior high school class before we went to Science: He was my first, startling experience with true genius, with his capacity to rapidly solve complex problems that, try as I might, took me forever. I talk about him earlier, in Chapter 10. He left Science after one year to go to an Ivy League college, which he soon quit to develop his own (over time, successful) business. That happened but was not as notable as it is today with school drop-outs like Bill Gates and Steve Jobs. But he, my former classmate, was gone, dead. By some grace of God, I was not.

Clyde Haberman, whose beat for the *New York Times* was for many years the City, was there, another member of the class of '62. Robert Strom also was in our graduating class. He had won the popular TV quiz show, *The $64,000 Question*, though many thought the program was rigged. He was very short (as were his wife and kids) and had gone on to work at IBM, doing brainy things.

There was a show of hands at the dinner reunion when the MC asked how many of us had artificial joints? Stents? Had taken LSD? Not that many, in answer to all three questions, though a lot more positive responses to the first two questions. Maybe some didn't want to admit their psychedelic trips, though I raised my hand in response to the third question—but not the first two.

An online survey (after all, this was Science) of the class taken before the reunion had 232 respondents. We were informed by the MC that 83 percent of us were currently married (many more than once); 81 percent had children; over 80 percent had graduate degrees (masters and doctorates); over 40 percent had undergone career changes; over 40 percent were retired. Many reported they had never planned to retire, and one said he would retire 10 years after he died, giving voice to my feelings exactly. An overwhelming number of alums reported feeling "very positive" about the school, endorsing that it made a "consequential difference" in their lives. I observed, during the recitation of these "data," and embodied in those alums in the room, what are the ingredients of successful aging: Being smart, from families that valued assimilation and hard work, well-educated, in long term relationships, and blessed with having lived in a society that believed in meritocracy—at least in New York City. As a result, we likely would be the winners of among the most precious of life's commodities—dignity, economic security, family, and community.

Bronx Science's graduating class had become, at the time of my 50th reunion, substantially Asian. This, in part, reflects the changing demographics of New York City and its ever-revitalizing immigrant communities. Whoever goes to Bronx Science today, or tomorrow, will discover that it is safe to be smart. They will experience that learning how to think and mastering skills and knowledge are immeasurable gifts that keep on giving. Imagine if that experience were one that could happen in any school in New York City or any other community in this vast nation?

Imagine if there were many, many more places like Science where it's possible to be able to *earn* standing in life, work, and community—and not just for the best students with the most intact and engaged of families. But for all our wondrous youth. Now, that would be something to be proud of.

Adapted from: A Safe Place to Be Smart: The Bronx High School of Science, The Huff Post, October 22, 2012 (Copyright Lloyd I Sederer).

*****

11A: Intelligence

Merriam-Webster defines intelligence as "the ability to learn or understand or to deal with new or trying situations; the ability to apply knowledge to manipulate one's environment or to think abstractly as measured by objective criteria (such as tests); mental acuteness."

Howard Gardner, one of America's great thinkers about education and learning, considered intelligence to be the capacity to solve problems, and then go on to considering the problems that *then* emerge, in a never-ending mental process that, over time, builds knowledge. Mastery too.

My grandmother used to say, after listening to someone, relative or not, who went on and on in a seemingly intelligent way that made no sense that he (or she) was "too smart for his own good." They lacked common sense, *sachel* in Yiddish, the invaluable quality that underlies all true intelligence. I have met quite a few people who are too smart for their own good; I find I don't have much time for them.

I prefer people who not only have common sense but also are problem solvers. That's a gift, and, if I dare say, an admirable dimension of intelligence. They take in information and use it to contribute to explaining and trying to solve the infinity of human dilemmas and difficulties we face as individuals, families, and communities. Those that spin yarn, so to speak, or worse try to fake or fool us, play fast and loose with the truth, won't get away with it forever. They will get what they deserve, which is not much, maybe not right away but in time as the arc of justice makes its way.

But when it comes to quantitatively measuring intelligence, producing a number with a ranking compared to others, the most popular tests include the *Stanford-Binet*, the *Wechsler* (*WAIS, WISC*), and the *IOWA*.

You can go online, Google *Stanford-Binet,* and subject yourself to 50 questions, a "quick" version—if you are wanting to feel bad that day about yourself. But the test itself, which I must have taken, is regarded as "reliable," a term that merely means that a person will score about the same over repeated administrations. Reliable is different from valid, which means it has the property of truly measuring what it purports to measure, in intelligence, and many other scientific domains. The completion of the full, standardized *Stanford-Binet* yields an Intelligence Quotient, IQ, held to be an important measure of we humans, if only in its five domains: reasoning, knowledge, quantitative abilities (like math), the capacity to process information visually and spatially, and working memory (that which is readily accessible and can be applied to problem-solving).

The *Stanford-Binet* has its roots in a French intelligence scale, fashioned by Alfred Binet and Theodore Simon. Its original function was to provide the French educational bureaucracy with a means to detect children with *limited* mental capacities. It was introduced in France in 1904 and adapted for use in this country a decade or so later, at Stanford University, hence its current name.

An IQ over 140 depicts "genius," but from what I have seen, you need to have a higher score to be a true genius. At 140, you probably are just really smart. "Average" is 90-109. Below 70 indicates what used to be called "mental retardation," now termed a developmental disability.

I recall getting my math and verbal scores at school, also summed for a combined score. There are also measures, respectively, of the "nonverbal" and "verbal" dimensions of the test. I did well, especially in math, which I suppose is why I got into The Bronx High School of Science. It was only later in life that I began to read a lot, which is vital for doing well on the verbal challenges. I guess I have developed in that area, given the volume and clutter of writings that I subject (willing) readers to.

The nonverbal test employs pictures, numbers, and symbols; the verbal employs words and reasoning. The verbal score has been a strong predictor of academic success in Western colleges and universities, so it helps with getting into a school if you have a high verbal score, not just a high math score. Often, the test taker will be more able, score higher, in one of these domains than the other. Those that achieve high scores in both are well equipped, at least cerebrally, to master the cognitive challenges of higher education.

Another well-known intelligence test is the *Wechsler*, for children and adults. Wechsler was a psychologist in mid-20th century America. The *WAIS* (*Wechsler [Adult] Intelligence Scale*) is for adults, duh, and the *WISC* for children. By the time I was no longer a child, the *WISC* was more popular than the *Stanford-Binet*, but it did not yield the inimitable IQ score. Its use was in children ranging from six to 16. It also measured two domains, namely verbal and performance, the latter by testing reasoning and picture completion. My son, Max, growing up in the '80s, had the *WISC*; like me, he scored better on performance (non-verbal skills like math). He's a very smart kid (though not a kid anymore, except sometimes, by mistake, in his dad's mind). Plus, he has plenty of *sachel*.

There is one more example of an intelligence test, which my wife tells me she took in the '70s in a public school in Connecticut. That's the *IOWA* Assessments. Which has its roots in that state but has since been more widely adopted nationally for children in grades K-12. The test's findings, over time, have been used to help refine educational methods (like lesson planning) as well determine an individual child's need for assistance, as well as their progress.

In other words, this nation—as do many others—has labored to reliably measure mental capabilities in children, and later as they mature as adults. Social circumstances and early childhood experience, not just biology, play very big roles in what youth or adults can bring to these intelligence exams, while the education they later have obtained (or not) further affects test results; with many showing disparities, not doing well in scores and thus, in opportunity.

But IQ is over-rated, I think. Unless, of course, you are developmentally delayed and thus suffer the great consequences of limited cognitive capacities.

You can also go online to have tested your "*Emotional Intelligence*," or Emotional Quotient (EQ), a concept advanced by Daniel Goleman. Could this be even more traumatic than getting your IQ? What does that mean, emotional intelligence? It is way more than good manners, but those go a long way in polite society.

The five areas identified in emotional intelligence are self-awareness, self-regulation, motivation, empathy, and social skills. There is an ongoing debate as to whether adults can improve their overall EQ, though adults can learn to better understand their emotions.

There are a variety of assessments available that can determine the EQ of children and adults, as well as be used to assess the organizational performance of a group, organization, or firm. There are still other tests that can create a profile of our brain functions, thereby to determine our top mental abilities, talents if you will, as well as how we routinely process information (known generally as our cognitive style). There are claims that a person bearing a higher EQ will perform better and earn more money at work, having been cognitively blessed with empathy, awareness, and the capacity to regulate feelings and actions. A high, composite EQ definitely comes in handy for enhancing work performance as well as fostering more meaningful and enduring relationships.

I think narcissistic people often have high levels of emotional intelligence. They use it, however, to engage, flatter, and manipulate others in order to serve *their own* needs. Like many things, how we use these attributes matters in the scheme of things, particularly regarding our morals, principles, and ethical conduct.

A notable derivative of emotional intelligence are the programs increasingly being introduced in school educational programs and curricula, around this and other countries, including in my home state of New York. These programs teach and advance childhood "social and emotional learning" (SEL). Often built into the core curriculum, SEL teaches critically needed developmental *skills*—including how to communicate with others, make decisions, respect others, problem solve, work as a team, and how to set goals. Few children are born with these skills, which are essential to personal growth and academic success; they also are preventative strategies, protective capacities in mental functioning, that reduce the risk of drug use and abuse, vital to beating the drug epidemic that has seized our country.

Is emotional intelligence an old wine in a new bottle? Is SEL a novel idea or school-based activity? My son went to a remarkable K-12 private school in Cambridge, Massachusetts, started by teachers almost a century ago to live up to their educational aspirations for their children: *The Shady Hill School*. If I am reincarnated as a human, I want to go to Shady Hill. The headmaster back then, Mr. Joe Seeger, a man physically disabled from the war (WWII) whose candor, stamina and resilience I admired, used to regularly hold large group, evening parent meetings. He would clearly and with passion tell us *how* to raise our kids—to talk with them, spend time with them, read to them, and invite their ideas and participation in decisions about the tasks of everyday life. There was nothing pedantic about his talks, which I welcomed, as did so many other parents. We, not just the students, were given instruction about how children best develop. No one had taught me, and I needed teaching. The kids themselves were attending a school that put a premium on their social and emotional learning, though it wasn't called that at the time. But there it was, in plain sight in the classrooms, fundamental to the culture, the essence, of what the school valued.

When my son was in the third grade at Shady Hill, I noticed he had no homework—unlike another nearby and notable private elementary school. I asked his homeroom teacher, why not? She referred me to Mr. Seeger. In his kind and wise way. he told me that the kids at Shady Hill, with whom the school maintained contact for their entire lives (whenever possible), had better rates of college admissions, to more competitive universities, and achieved greater professional success than did the students at that nearby school. He was not boasting. Simply providing academic and career facts, which he implied speak for themselves. There was, of course, the wonderful humanity of the school's gentility he also was professing. I subsequently learned that Shady Hill had 100% alumni donations, even if only $1, every year since the distant past. That means to me that the alumni, not just the parents, wanted to help support the school, whatever their means, to "pay forward" the kindness they had received. It was not just competency and advantage they had built, but the values they had been exposed to and adopted.

At Science, like at Stuyvesant High School and many private secondary schools, there exist a collection of youth with high IQs (though not necessarily high EQs). Most come from homes without violence, with no active addiction or untreated serious mental illnesses. Homes where a premium is placed on learning, on education—the great leveler, the best gateway to a career and financial security. For youth growing up in poverty, with food and housing insecurity, with domestic violence or the ravages of untreated substance or mental disorder, or growing up in the foster care system, they seldom have the same shot at a good education, and are thus more prone to troubles, scholastically and personally.

The public schools of the 1950s, in most states like mine, were for those of modest and middle-class financial standing, the *principal* route to a life better than one's parents, at least economically and professionally. Emotional life is another matter. Public education today faces a vast erosion of resources and culture: too many good teachers leaving for other, better-paying jobs; disruptive school "climates," where order is hard to maintain and bullying is common; visible difficulties in the capacity for teachers and school administrators to sustain respect and civility among the students; in curricula that do not encompass social and emotional learning; by unsafe environments (at school, at home, and in the neighborhoods). Schools, sadly, now have to practice "shooting drills" as a result of horrific violence, with regular news headlines reporting on yet another mass murder. I can't imagine how this can enhance student and school performance.

Evaporating across this great country, famed for its opportunities, is the chance for an equitable, decent education. We are still leaving children "behind," not giving them the experience of the wonders of learning and a deep sense of community. We are, thus, often foreclosing their hopes and likelihood of future success (in all its economic and psychic dimensions). That need not continue to happen. We all have the opportunity, the obligation I think, to act locally as responsible citizens, and give today's children the chances some of us had. For today's youth to learn while still young, and for all of us to be nurtured and sustained by lifelong learning.

*****

Chapter 12
Savin Business Machines

Though I didn't think about it much, like my father I should have been destined to take over the family business. First, it was a grocery store, then a supermarket, then a small stationery store, and finally an office supply company. I had done some odd, quite limited jobs in the supermarket because I was still too young (if you don't count looking after my sister, three years younger). But I had worked in the stationery store, Depot Stationers in Tuckahoe, New York, north of the city since I was eight. Weekends, some holidays, but not the summers. Maybe that was time off for good behavior? The summers were for camp and then my uncle Ben's chicken farm in Walden, New York, with my cousins, mother, and aunt, and their husbands (my father and uncle) coming on the weekends when chores seemed to eclipse the idleness and calm of the weekdays.

In May of my junior year in high school, I was going to turn 16. That meant I would be legal to work, and not just as a kid in his dad's store. I could get a Social Security card!

Unbeknownst to me, my father had spoken with one of his regular customers, Mr. Max Low (introduced earlier), who came into the store on weekends to buy newspapers, greeting cards, and magazines. One day, a Saturday in the spring while I was working there, my father introduced me to Mr. Low, a short, finely dressed older man. Very distinguished looking, rich too it turned out. Mr. Low gave me a business card and said I should come to see him at his office, in Manhattan. I imagined my father had determined I was not worth trying to save, that I had done too much wrong, or was such a nuisance that it was time to farm me out. Or, maybe, he had arranged for me to be put into a transatlantic shipping carton (like Mr. Low used in his business), captured upon my visit with Mr. Low and shipped out of the country?

Didn't happen, at least not yet.

When I went to see Mr. Low in a tall, formidable building in mid-town Manhattan, I waited in his secretary's office, outside of his. He owned any number of businesses, I had been told by my father, including a hospital supply company. He was a business magnate, Jewish too.

After a short wait, I was told by his secretary to go in. I pulled myself out of the leather waiting room chair and entered his chambers. He had a huge desk and sat behind it smiling. "Sit down," he said. He told me my father said I was a smart kid, and a hard worker too. My dad had told him more about me than he ever told me. If I wanted, that summer when school was out, he could arrange for me to have a job in his son-in-law's new business, Savin Business Machines. The warehouse and office were in Lower Manhattan, but I could get there by subway.

I whispered, "Sure." I had no idea what this all meant, but I was in no position to ask a lot of questions or say no. The meeting, such as it was, probably lasted five minutes.

But I was awed by him, his office, his elegance, and the opportunity he was offering.

Not long after that, my father got a call—he informed me one evening—about how I could then apply for this mysterious, and geographically distant job (at least it was in NYC, not in Maine or New Hampshire). My dad did not tell me what the job was, I suspect he also didn't know. But he told me where and when I needed to go for my interview.

Orders in hand, I dutifully reported, on a day free from school, in the spring, to the offices of Savin Business Machines. It was a long subway ride, starting above-ground on Gun Hill Road with the Dyre Avenue Line, which was then running in the North Bronx. I needed to change trains for the White Plains Road Line and finally switch to the IRT Third Avenue Line. I exited, surfacing from the no longer above-ground train, on Grand Street. It was a short walk to a tall, vintage New York, cream-colored building on the Lower East Side of Manhattan, not so far from the famed (at least in my family) Orchard Street, but more industrial. There was a small, public park across the street where I briefly plunked myself down to gather courage.

Savin, according to the building directory in the lobby, occupied the ground as well as an upper floor. I headed to the upper floor, the office, as I had been instructed. I was to meet with the business manager, not Mr. Bob Savin, the owner and entrepreneur, also Mr. Low's son-in-law. Elise Lorenz (*let's call her that*) greeted me. She was a stunningly handsome, fair-haired woman, probably in her early forties. German stock, with a tiny accent. I thought she looked like Ingrid Bergman in her later movies. I think I probably developed a crush on her, at that very moment.

She told me somethings about Savin. About its ambition to be a leading business machine company (copying and fax machines, and the like) in this country. I tried to pay attention, but it was hard. I was anxious, surrounded by novelty, and infused with adolescent testosterone and desire for this gorgeous woman. I did hear her say, a bit later, that I could start as soon as I got a Social Security card and school was over. Thank you very much.

I reported for work on a late June day, a Monday, when the customary business week begins. I went up to the office. Elise, as she wanted to be called, told me to go downstairs, I would be starting in the warehouse. There, George (*let's call him that*), a tall, muscular and gentlemanly black man told me to just follow him around for a while. It was just him and one other man, and now me, hardly a step forward in manpower. George was the warehouse foreman, which meant he did most of the work. Now he also had to take care of me. I thought, not fair. I foreswore to myself I would try to be useful.

I learned how to package machines and paper for shipping, to address labels, and to receive boxes, deliveries on the rear loading dock, and store them in their proper places. It was heavy work, hot down there too. But it felt good, doing labor, not exactly construction, but still being on task, responsibly and quickly, like business should be done. I got to know their inventory and whom they bought from and sold to. I ate ravenously like I must have weighed at least 300 pounds (I probably weighed under 150 pounds). George was devoted to Elise, as was I. Maybe he had a crush on her too.

After a few weeks, Elise said I should come work in the office. Maybe that was planned, or maybe she was more short-handed there. My main job was reconciling bills and payments. There were sheets and sheets of paper with numbers that had to be compared and an adding machine for me to total all kinds of columns. I was good at math, maybe not so much theoretical calculus, but arithmetic – adding, subtracting, and calculations, which were helped a lot by a machine. I was detail-oriented and could keep my mind from wandering, which had always come in handy in school. In short, I was doing my job, getting through the piles, no problem. From time to time, Elise thanked me for my work. It felt like a heavenly touch.

I would spend my lunch hours in the park (when there wasn't pouring rain) blissfully alone, eating a sandwich I had brought or something I bought from a nearby deli. Not half as much food as when I was in the warehouse, but still more than I could eat today without getting as big as a house. I read books, science and science fiction. After all, I was a student at Bronx Science.

I wore a plain, long-sleeved shirt and khakis; those were my office uniform. No tie. While others in the office were friendly, they knew I was temporary, not going to last long, so I was mostly ignored by them. Except for Elise, who was like a caring but demanding aunt. From time to time, Mr. Savin would pass by in the general office area, sometimes give me a nod, that's about it; what he knew about me, I don't know. I was the beneficiary of his father-in-law's largesse, and hopefully acquitting his decision by proving myself useful.

After endless subway rides, made a bit timeless by doing the daily NY Herald Tribune crossword, the end of August loomed. High school was to start again, in the Bronx. One day, during my last week at Savin Business Machines, Elise asked if she could take me out to lunch. I just about passed out. We went to a small, simple, Greek restaurant not far from the office. She asked me about school, my plans for college, my career interests—all of which had to be totally boring, but she seemed to be listening and said some encouraging things. I imagined I was at lunch with a movie star, who had inexplicably and curiously taken an interest in me. Skinny, Jewish, bespectacled me. Then we had to go back to work. On Friday, my last day, she firmly shook my hand and wished me well. I never saw her again. Savin Business Machines, the company, did well, for some time, then I think it was bought out by a bigger fish in that ocean. I should have bought stock when it went public.

I recall the pride I had in working hard, and not for my father. For getting a paycheck, paying into Social Security (which I now collect), for venturing to Lower Manhattan, to seeing a world far broader than my family and my family's business. My mother often asked about my day, but my father, in his inimitable, far off way, seemed not to care. He had his own business to worry about.

I was becoming a New Yorker, not just a kid from the Bronx. And I was exiting from my family and the family business. Unlike my father, who toiled in his father's South Bronx grocery store and took over when his dad died, I was being released to the outer world. The introduction to Max Low was my father's way of saying I was free to go. He

177

never expected me to take over the family business. That job ultimately fell to my sister's husband, an attorney in the NYC DA's office, who had the really tough job of working for my dad, though he would learn a lot. I was on the path to a life as a student, who would become what every Jewish mother wants her son to be—a doctor.

*****

12A: Working, but Not for Your Family

I don't know if it is better, worse, or both? I mean, working for your family or for someone else, not a relation.

By the time I was eight, into my mid-teens, the early '50s to the early '60s, I had worked in my father's businesses. I also had worked (like *really* worked as in labored) summers on my uncle Ben's Walden, New York, farm—unpaid of course, cleaning chicken coops, cutting hedges and lawns, and tending a large garden (more on this in Chapter 14). On the Walden farm, I felt a bit like a migrant worker, perhaps never to be free until I could escape. Yet, to give credit where it is due, I got to spend summers outside of NYC, and learn the skills of shooting a rifle, as well as horseback riding and gardening, which otherwise would never have happened. More about my uncle Ben and that later on.

There are responsibilities—and rewards—inherent to being a part of a family. Families give and they take. It's a two-way street, I now believe, though I wouldn't have said that as a child, with my concerns and attention overwhelmingly focused on guess who. Yet I survived, despite my worries to the contrary. Turns out, I see now, no child has ever died from having responsibilities, from giving (while necessarily also being given to, because if not, that is neglect and drills a big hole in a person) and contributing. The full swirl of life in a functional and loving family. This a view I had to learn and build into the family I would create on my own: Just ask my son (and step-son). A family works when everyone does their part.

My world until Savin Business Machines had been awfully insular—family, family business, the Bronx, public and Hebrew school, a few friends, some books, and lots of television. A job inside the family generally does not induce an appreciation for the family business, because of its centrality in supporting the family and ensuring its economic security. A family business seems awfully obligatory: There is no negotiation to be had, just figuratively climb on board the moving train and start shoveling its furnaces with coal. Or removing snow in front of the store, or assembling newspapers (see the opening story of this memoir). Kids simply are too young to understand. Their brains need to myelinate, to mature, and that takes well over 20 years to happen. But a job working for someone other than a father (or mother, or close relative), and being a bit older, has its different calculus. You are even expected to behave like an adult, even if you fake it.

At Savin, I had no idea what to expect, what they would want me to do. No clue what their performance expectations were for me except what I was told to do from day to day. Those were the quotidian tasks, but what about more? How might I actually assist in and contribute to the goals of an organization; what fuels and sustains a company and its personnel?

The "management" didn't know who I was—except that I was a teenager from a Jewish family at a school for smart kids—and that their *actual* boss, the family patriarch, Max Low, had said, "Give this kid a job." I certainly did not know who these strangers were, not one of them: the manager, the president of the company, and fellow workers. Like a job in the real world, outside the family, typically entails. Yet I did realize, probably could not articulate, that acceptance in any role, station, position of trust, or responsibility in another's enterprise must be earned. That means being industrious, intelligent, efficient, and trying not to be an interpersonal *clutz*, a social maladroit. Any pride of place and sense of achievement had to be earned by a job well done, and behaving like a grown-up, not as a child in a nuclear family.

There were workers in my father's businesses. Quite a few in the supermarket. There were fewer, at first, in the stationery business (until it became a company, but I was by then long gone and into medical school). The relationship of the employees with my father was complex: some were there simply for the pay to cover their rent, some to strive for vocational advancement, to better realize the American dream of upward mobility, some for both. There were those who were proud of their work, however repetitive, those seeking recognition by being given greater job responsibilities, as well as higher wages. My father was a tough but fair boss. He worked harder than anyone else; not intentionally, upon reflection, to set a standard for others but because that was his nature. I know where I got that from. He hired across racial lines, not so common back then in small businesses, even in the New York City area. But he was the boss, and I was his son. I was not about to be fired for sleeping on the job, or reading comic books, not that I did so much of either of those. But, to be honest, I was not above those indolent activities.

When I started at Savin Business Machines, I had to learn the hierarchy, who made decisions, who had authority. Usually, that is plain, but not always, especially when the owner is regularly absent, engaged in work outside the office, when ownership is shared with a partner, or when a trusted person (but not the owner) is put in charge of day to day operations. How a group of co-workers, not related by blood, got along, or not, was a dynamic to be observed, understood, and adapted to. To succeed as workers, for the business to succeed, we all needed to acclimate successfully to the work setting, and each other. Today, skills like these are sometimes called "emotional intelligence." There are personality inventories, like the *Myers Briggs*, that help workers, not only in professional jobs, know their own character style and those of colleagues (like extroversion and introversion, thinking and feeling), which can be used to be more effective, instead of complaining or railing against the person at the next desk or work table. But back then, I learned that success meant getting along, paying attention, and doing what you were told, with no help from training workshops or job coaches.

I discovered quickly who was in charge of the office, warehouse, and everyday business at Savin. Elise. She was crisp and clear in her manner and expectations. Having someone clearly and ably in charge is not always the case; sometimes, leadership is in the hands of someone not quite up to the job, which fosters worker problems and workarounds. When ambiguity reigns, dysfunction abounds, and blame usually is around the corner. I like clarity, most people do. Those given to chaos and impulsivity can be ruinous to a business, not only to the government of a nation.

Being a temporary employee carries with it, as well, little social standing in the work community: here one day, gone to "better" things tomorrow (like school). Some people are generous in their responses to a transient co-worker, such as I was, some were not. Some fair, some not. Some truthful, some not. That's life, as the song goes.

We are fortunate when those kindnesses happen in a family. It's a blessing, not to be expected or relied upon, when that happens in work (and school) situations, where the vagaries of the setting and people require bending to the personality of the boss and other co-workers. Otherwise, the common purpose can't be achieved, and essential business goals become elusive. I did not know if Elise, my boss at Savin Business Machines, had children, no less a husband. But I quickly realized that if I measured up, did my job well, quickly and with decorum, she would treat me fairly, even with solicitude, and teach me, my summer tenure notwithstanding. I was lucky.

I recall another summer, a couple of years later, where I held two jobs: One was loading 18-wheeler truck cabs during the graveyard shift in a Brooklyn warehouse (where my two best friends also worked, but we were not alongside each another); it was a big place and we filled in for other, stronger, more competent workers. My other job was as a lowest level server (the busboy) at a fancy, Westchester golf course, in a clubhouse that looked like a mansion. It offered French service (which means too many people waiting hand and foot on the diners).

What mattered at both jobs had nothing to do with me personally, a developing young man in need of substantial guidance and support, but how fast I could load the trucks, without damaging property, and how obsequious and tidy I could be with the restaurant patrons. I truly did not like these jobs. No culture of community and support was anywhere to be found. Though they paid well. The better of the two was the truck depot, which paid in cash at the end of each shift, enough money to be able to waste some of it at the food truck parked outside the warehouse. For all I know, I was not a legal worker there, and it surely wasn't a union shop.

These settings, where a person is anonymous, invisible, with little or no voice and an uncertain future, were, I discovered, more the rule than the exception. Back then and no different today. Enlightened bosses, even supervisors, are a modern idea, which typically relies on the character of individuals, not the ambient culture of an organization, despite what may be its manifest pronouncements or slogans.

Yet even in the most rote of jobs, how a person is regarded, and their views considered, makes a difference for the productivity and success of an enterprise. The fellow who drove the truck that delivered merchandise for my father's stationery store stayed with that job for more than two decades; he was always reliable and trustworthy. He likely brought those qualities to his job from day one, but they were supported so they were sustained, I believe because he felt respected and equitably treated. Too often, the inequities, the financial and social disparities, between owner and worker are big, even vast, now more so than ever—especially regarding earnings.

As a doctor, I have had the privilege of clinically heading a variety of treatment, research, and public health programs, including a Harvard teaching hospital, a municipal and state government agency, the latter with over a score of public hospitals and hundreds of doctors and thousands of nurses and aides.

One thing I have learned is that money is *not* the top priority for medical professionals. Not that they don't need good pay to cover large college and medical school debt (averaging near to $200,000 per graduate) and the costs of living, home and car ownership, and educating their children. But good doctors and nurses, as well as other health professionals, want to serve, to care for those they are privileged to be asked to help.

We all benefit from and respond to working in a learning environment, where skills and knowledge are fostered and our ideas count, where we receive respect (which still must be earned), and where advancement is possible because a meritocracy prevails. Treat professionals and other caregivers right, and they will treat patients, families, colleagues, and their bosses right. These are essential working conditions for medical settings—to better ensure safety and quality care and to treat patients and families humanely. Good, effective leadership understands these elements of a work environment—and that they must be consistently delivered, not just politically correct slogans or trying to avert unionization. But to make services and an organization hum.

Work can enable us to escape tedium and dreariness (most of the time) when it is enlivened by a sense of purpose. Purpose is possible across countless endeavors, family or otherwise. It is by no means singular to professionals, though we tend to find more sense of purpose among educated people doing white-collar jobs (or in uniform). Those legions of people who make hospitals and clinics (my métier), for example, safe, sanitary, welcoming, and caring can, often do, experience a sense of purpose, not only the doctors or nurses. We all can achieve a sense of purpose when we know we are contributing to our family, to a family business, which was an essential ingredient in my home life. And beyond that nuclear haven, to where and when we contribute to the community; a government (including the military, as well as police, firefighters and other first responders) or private organization; a company (for-profit or not-for profit, or a charity); a house of faith; and when the recipients of our efforts palpably benefit from our services or products. Purpose fosters a sense of meaning, a reason for living.

Meaning and purpose have long been fundamental to faith-based organizations. While religious institutions seem to be eroding in this country (though hardly all nations), people of faith, foot soldiers for belief, are everywhere, though to see them, we now need to look more carefully or ask. Professionals are buoyed when they serve a purpose, in health, education, safety, law and law enforcement, government, the armed forces, and so on. When the experience of purpose fades or is trampled on by the exigencies of financial pressures, cause dims and resolve weakens. These are hard to regain.

Of course, these notions apply equally to many other forms of work and contribution, including farmers and builders, those who feed and house us, those that tend to our needs, small and grave, those who keep supply chains going and energy delivered, and many, many other occupations. There is no monopoly on purpose, no corner to its market nor a set limit in its quantity, and no geographical boundaries to being its beneficiaries.

Work, inside and outside of family businesses, remains an enduring source of purpose and meaning—when done well, honestly, and serves others. Its oxygen can be there for all of us to breathe when we are engaged in a life of contribution.

*****

Chapter 13
My First Car

I bet you never heard of a DeSoto? Nor had I—and I was around when they were made. Chrysler started manufacturing them in 1928 and abandoned the brand in 1960. It was 1962, my last year of high school, at the tender age of 17, when I formally met a DeSoto.

I had passed my driving test the year before. Aged 16, and dying to drive, even if I would be a menace on the road. The test official must have had a good night before since he decided I was no more dangerous than the next guy, or gal. I thought for sure I first would fail the eye test, not the letters and numbers but the color chart. I was (am) color blind, especially red-green colorblindness. Green defies me, I can barely detect it, only when of a very deep hue and then I can't tell it from brown. I could tell the difference in a traffic light because the red looked darker, surely different from the green, which looked white to me. For those of you now fearing meeting me on the road, I have never run a red light—except intentionally (as it was changing). To my amazement, I saw the correct image, a number buried in the maze of dots, on the color chart. I had overcome what I feared would be my greatest barrier to getting a driving license, and would be allowed to take the road test

Becoming a driver starts with a learner's permit. This means someone had to teach me to drive—to sit next to me as I endangered their life, not just those of other motorists or pedestrians. That was my dad since my mother would have been way too terrified and usually had trouble controlling me. Dad was the default mode when it came to dealing with me, when talking sense to me had been exhausted.

One Sunday, my father decided to take me out for a driving lesson. I made countless circles and practiced parking in a vast parking lot not far from our home in the Bronx. The next time, it was onto the Bronx streets; it would be a long time before I would be allowed to drive in Manhattan. But my favorite time "learning" to drive was when my dad's good friend, Larry (and his wife), came over to visit. They lived in Fort Lee, New Jersey, right over the GW Bridge. Larry owned a wholesale children's (cheap) clothing import business in the Garment District of Lower Manhattan. He cursed and told dirty and tasteless jokes all the time, which both my dad loved – me too. Around him, I felt like my testosterone and bad sense of humor both were being put to some use.

Larry liked to drink. I think he must have been a bit of a drinker since a half bottle of Chivas scotch would be gone after he visited, with no discernable effects, except on the volume in the bottle. My father really liked him; Larry made him laugh, which was not a common practice for my dad. Larry was going to let me drive his big Buick, four-door with white-walled tires, as he sat in the passenger seat and took a nap. I went on highways, into the City (Manhattan that is), everywhere. I had no idea where I was going: there were no Google directions on a smartphone and no screen on the forward center dashboard; it would be decades before those arrived. Plus, of course, I had seriously limited skills at the wheel. Yet, only a few times did he rouse and gasp, maybe due to another car blasting its horn at my driving. But that was no reason for quitting the outing. Soon, again, he would be fast asleep.

Before I became old enough to drive on my own, still 17, on one of our regular visits to Queens to visit my mother's sister, Muriel, and her family, my father drove me to my uncle Ben's (her husband, the same uncle who had the chicken farm in Walden, NY) auto-body repair and paint shop. The kind you see that has a dangling metal sign and beat-up steel doors in sketchy neighborhoods. After being a Navy pilot instructor in the war, Uncle Ben opened this shop. I guess he knew a lot about mechanical things, not just planes. My dad had talked with Ben about his finding me a car. I am not sure he was the best person to ask, but it would be cheap.

Upon my dad's and my arrival at Ben's shop, he proudly said he had found me a car. A 1955 DeSoto. Two-toned, if you tried hard to see the colors. With small fins and smaller, round brake lights. We went into the work area of his shop, where it was parked, to inspect it, which is surely overstating our position. The engine started reluctantly. The car's body looked like it had been left exposed in Mojave Desert conditions for 100 years. The mileage gauge was broken, probably from having exceeded all limits.

I asked my uncle if he would paint it. After all, he did run a paint shop too. I was even more out of it then than I am today. I should have known better from my time under his rule when we spent summers on his Walden, New York chicken farm (see the final chapter on chickens, etc.). Ben didn't bother answering my question about painting the car; it was as if I had asked him if he wanted some deer ticks or venereal disease. He went further inside, deep into the shop, and came out with a stubby, lidded can of "compound" (much like wax, though more abrasive). I knew the term "compound" from math and chemistry, but this kind of compound was novel to me. Even more novel, and alarming, was his saying I should get some rags and rub this stuff all over the exterior, then rub it on some more, until I could see the paint. He offered no more counsel. For $50, I was the owner of a DeSoto, my first car. The compound was free. I paid him, cash of course, from my earnings as an employee at Savin Business Machines.

Both the car and my driving made it back from Queens to the Bronx. I parked it in the narrow driveway of our 3-decker house. I immediately got some rags and started to apply the compound. This was not like rubbing Mediterranean seasoning paste on codfish. Or Vaseline on chapped lips. This was like digging a 3x10 foot trench, in terms of pure, hard labor. The weather was warm, and I sweated like in a Turkish Bath. It took over a week, after school and on the weekend, whenever it was not raining. The two-tones of its blue exterior had become just about visible to the naked eye. A lot of the rust was gone. I can't say the paint shined, but it looked pretty good to me. Besides, I had had enough of that rubbing. My arms and shoulders seemed to have sizably grown as if I took anabolic steroids; though, in fact, it had to be from their unremitting labor on the car's exterior. I had my first car, retrieved by Uncle Ben from who knows where and given a reprieve from the scrap heap—at least for the moment. I wish I had taken before and after photos, if anything to prove this story.

There is something about not just driving a car your family has but having your own. The youthful pride I had was a joy. It didn't need to be new, or expensive, or a sporty sedan. Not even a Corvette, though I wouldn't have turned one of those down.

I remember driving the DeSoto to my first day of classes at City College in Northern Manhattan. It was September of 1962. Parking was possible then, with no meters either. I turned off the engine. I walked away from the car, my car, admiring its off-kilter beauty, leaving it there on the street in Harlem, confident that no one would bother to steal it.

*****

13A: Cars

My step-grandson, my wife's son's older son, was three years old as I write about him here. His name is Oscar. He has at least one hundred toy cars, trucks, fire engines, ambulances, and earth-moving machines. In a rainbow of colors and sizes, from those that fit in his little paw to those nearing in length his height. Their wheels turn, and doors open and close. Some make sounds or have flashing lights. He never leaves the house without one, usually two; more than two are usually too hard to carry. He can pleasurably spend hours, every day, playing with these vehicles.

I guess you would say my first car was not the DeSoto I tenderly describe above. It must have been a toy car, a miniature of real life, those around when I was his age, which was a long time ago. Though I assure you, there were cars. Planes too, which could fly from New York City to Europe; however, they couldn't cross the Atlantic without refueling in Gander, in the Canadian counties of Newfoundland and Labrador. If you don't know about Gander, you haven't seen *Come from Away*, the amazingly uplifting Broadway show. Which, may I say, could be a great pleasure ahead for you. Try not to miss it, even if you don't care for musicals.

One day, my DeSoto started choking, then just stopped, died, on an off-ramp of the Bruckner Expressway. It was hopeless to try to resuscitate it, plus I could recover its cost (recall that was $50) by selling it to a tow truck owner who could offload it for scrap metal, maybe extract some motor parts as well.

The next in my cavalcade of motor vehicles was an old Oldsmobile, two-doored and two-toned (at some past time), maybe issued a few years after the DeSoto, with the odometer miles surely tampered with, since they were not even in the tens of thousands. We—my father and I—got this one on a used-car lot in the Bronx; I am not suggesting this be the kind of place where you might go, it was just convenient for my father and cheap for me. It had more panache than the DeSoto; after all, it was an "Olds," a car with some distinction at the time.

I did a far more cursory job of compounding the Oldsmobile. With my second car, I didn't really care so much about its appearance. Plus, it had less body damage and decay, maybe only the equivalent of 50 years of exposure to brutal desert winds. It lasted less than a year. At least it didn't poop out on a highway, bridge, or blocking a traffic exit. One day, in front of our Eastchester Street home, the Olds simply would not start. Charging the battery with those red, dangerous cables was of no use. True to its name, it was old. It was beyond automotive 'CPR'.

It was time for a new car. I was in college, beyond the era of this memoir, and had been accumulating cash from all my jobs and had barely any expenses since I lived at my parents' home and had no tuition (well, maybe there was $30-40 a year in fees at City College). I did have to buy books and gas. I had earned enough from those years working, plus some modest poker winnings, to buy a new car, though I still needed cash from my dad (I thought he would require a loan; he was big on self-reliance, but he didn't). I—probably my dad—decided to buy a bottom-of-the-line *Mercury Comet* (bet you never heard of that one either). Yellow. I have no idea what factored into that choice. Maybe, and I don't recall, it was the cheapest on the dealer's lot (also in the Bronx), because no one wanted that make or model, in its bright, awful yellow. It may have cried out "lemon!" given its color.

But now, however, probably because of its eye-catching color, I did worry a bit that my new car would be deservedly defaced when I parked it away from home. It might be stolen—on a lark, not because there could be any resale value from the automotive parts, since, well, they were machinery for a *Mercury Comet*. It might, however, invite trouble since it stood decidedly out of place at a curbside on Amsterdam Avenue, near my college. But that never happened. I became the "designated" driver on weekend nights when my City College pals and I went out, as I was the only one with a car. We frequently went to the West End Bar on Broadway, near Columbia University. I would mostly forego the drinking and smoking weed that was intrinsic to those evenings.

The *Comet* lasted until my college graduation in 1966, well beyond the time horizon of this memoir's meanderings. I was going off to medical school, in Upstate New York. I traded in that rather odd choice of a driving machine, now a dull yellow with lots of body wounds from its NYC existence, and bought my first (used) Volkswagen Beetle, a mid-hue blue as I recall. There was no flower holder in the dash (to contain a faux, stemmed something or the other); that cute innovation was far off in the future. I was leaving New York City, and my parade of early, no-way cool, but useful cars behind. My car purchases continued, but their tale will not be told here.

What do you imagine is the best-selling vehicle in America today? It's a trick question because it is not a car. The Kelly "Blue Book" reports that 17.2 million cars and trucks were sold in the US in 2017. Of these, the top-selling vehicle was one of Ford Motor Company's F-Series: The F-150s. Trucks! Pick-up trucks, that is.

Ford reports the F-150s have towing capacities on a gradient from 7,700 lbs., to 9,100 lbs., to 11,600 lbs., to a bruising maximum of 13,200 lbs.—more than the weight of a fully-grown elephant. You can get the standard V6 engine or buy the more powerful "EcoBoost." This truck has 18" "Heavy Duty" wheels. This is all Greek to me since I have never owned a truck, nor sought to carry a heavy payload in one. A person like me could get a hernia loading or unloading it. The sales of Chevrolet Silverados and Dodge Rams, by the way, trail the Ford trucks by a lot.

There are not many trucks where I now live, in an urban area. That's if you don't count panel trucks, which are ubiquitous eye-sores, especially in New York City. They all seem to have similar dents, dings, and scratches, badges of vehicular courage, along with their paint crusting off. Their vintage often seems decades old, timeless. They are the weary beasts that transport workers and materials around the boroughs, or to and from New Jersey. Some of these trucks declare a company name, some add an address or phone number, some even a website. Some are barren of any identification, maybe because they don't care for more business, or are doing something clandestine or unlawful. Those blank, unmemorable beasts carry the message, I infer, "Don't ask."

Not for any real function, I can discern, there are oodles of SUVs in New York (and many other cities). Riding high on their suspensions, with massive, deeply treaded tires, they easily can handle any floodwaters that might arise from a broken, gushing fire hydrant. For drivers of ordinary cars, the SUVs block the view ahead, adding to a person's agitation when caught in traffic and wanting to see what's happening ahead; what's paralyzing the flow of vehicles, especially mine, in pursuit of their respective destinations. You are blindfolded to the action ahead unless you get out the driver's door to peer, which is apt to be more dangerous than climbing Everest – given the ire of nearby drivers.

The best-selling cars in the US (cars, not trucks, as elucidated above) are a variety of lower-cost, fuel-efficient imports, like the Toyota Camrys and Corollas, the Honda Civics, Kias, and Chevy Equinoxes. In the northeast, there seem to be a fair number of Hyundais. All very practical but tending to lack in style, to be boring members of the urban automotive life: they vanish into the vehicular landscape, like boulders on a mountainside. They are hard to tell apart. More and more models are hybrids, and some electric (though these cost more money).

Cars seem more so to be the obsession of men (carrying forth their mesmerization from boyhood). Not just as ways to get places but as ways to change a man's frame of mind. "Muscle" cars, with immense engines, fierce lines, and reaching almost supersonic speeds in a matter of seconds must have some appeal to the Y chromosome, to the XY pairing that makes for boys, not XX like girls. For me, included. More so than a luxury Mercedes, Lexus, or Audi, which are surely more comfortable to ride in.

Even *Disney* in its spate of animated films has capitalized on cars, car stories, not just toy stories, with voices supplied by huge Hollywood stars. I wonder if these films draw more boys than girls?

My step-grandson, whose car story introduced this essay, recently went to a *Monster Truck Jam* (an outdoor truck show). Live on the track, I was informed by him and his dad, were an astonishing assortment of big and small trucks, with cabs sitting six feet above their gigantic tires, decked out in fabulous colors and with countless decals (mostly advertising things to drink or buy). The trucks raced against one another, flew through the air after accelerating up steeply inclined sections of track, and dutifully crashed into one another, with no evident human casualties. Oscar (that's his name, in case you didn't remember) was awed. The thrill (I saw on video) on that boy's face extended from ear to ear, a feeling to be envied. He had to wear earphones to mute the roar of the trucks and the crowd. The moment that transfixed him the most, in fact, was when one disabled truck, hopelessly lying on its side, had to be rescued, dragged off the motorway, by a tow truck. I think he is more apt to become a caregiver than a race driver or mechanic.

*****

Chapter 14
Chickens, Hedges, and
Public Service

When I was about eight, maybe nine years old, my family—
my parents, my sister Marge (three years younger), and I—
started spending a month or more each summer at my
uncle's chicken farm in Walden, New York. *Not* to be
confused with Walden Pond, nor my uncle with Thoreau,
the legendary American author of the mid-1800s.

Improbable as it was, my uncle Ben, married to my
mother's younger sister, Muriel, who owned and ran an auto
body repair and paint shop in Queens (detailed earlier), had
bought a sprawling chicken farm near Newburgh, New
York, a few hours' drive from the city, near the Catskill
Mountains.

My uncle's farm had two vast chicken coops, each of
which stretched for what seemed like three football fields,
though each was more likely less than half the length of one.
I was small, so big is relative. In each coop, hundreds of
chickens clucked and squawked. They ran about on a wire
mesh net so their frequent chalky droppings fell to the
ground some three feet below. Their huge poop bin, if you

will, was accessible by a number of small, squat doors spaced along the coop's lower panels. The chickens, hens, in fact, laid their brown eggs, one of the two ways they contributed to the table and the economy of the farm, in carefully positioned wall-build roosts in the coop. The eggs thus could be harvested above ground on a walkway built into the coop, without having to walk on the net or among the chickens. Groveling beneath the net was what I and my cousin Steve, who was tougher than me, had to do to reduce the endlessly accumulating pile of chicken shit.

My aunt Muriel or her daughter, my older cousin Rita, would collect the eggs each morning, take them to the basement of the house, and "candle" them, shining the light from an incandescent bulb into the egg to determine if it had been inseminated. I have no idea how the roosters got to the hens, but nature usually finds a way. Only the unfertilized eggs were eaten or sold. It was my cousin Steve's and my job, as the older of the three boys ensnared on the farm, to regularly clear away their droppings so they wouldn't rise to a level that could engulf and entomb the hapless chickens in their own excretions. My cousin Alan, Steve's brother, was too young and too small to do this kind of hard labor. What good was he? He got away with murder.

That was well over 60 years ago, so I doubt much was known about the toxic qualities of chicken shit. Even if that might have arcanely be known by agricultural science experts at Cornell, in Ithaca, NY, my uncle Ben surely had not known or sought out that information. Even if he did, I don't think it was going to get in his way, nor would he tell his wife or my mother. After all, the job needed to be done. Just in case you wonder, chicken excrement had not been a subject my cousin or I had studied in science classes in New York City public schools. So, we didn't wear face masks; those were for tear gas or to defy chemical weapons (or coronavirus today). But thinking about it now, there had to be some terrible toxicity, like in a chemical weapon outlawed by The Geneva Convention, from what we were breathing from the chicken droppings. Today, I feel fortunate that neither my brain or lungs were irrevocably damaged by the incredibly caustic stuff we shoveled and hauled. Nor did Steve and I suffer evident orthopedic damage from the hours of stooping to muck out the coops until there was sufficient space for the chickens to continue their daily business. We were young, our joints and back were more resilient then.

A small amount of what we collected served as manure for the farm's huge garden, which we weeded and watered (when rain did not come). But not much of the chicken poop served this worthy gardening purpose since there were cows and horses in neighboring farms and thus plenty of the type of manure that really gets vegetables and fruits, including the grape arbor, to grow as if they were amply dosed with *Miracle Grow* (which by the way was not around then).

In addition to the coops and garden, there was no shortage of other chores for we boys to do, again just the two of us more grown child laborers. The farm's long, curving driveway was bordered on both sides by hedges. Each felt a mile long—though they likely were also about half a football field in length. The hedges were on our list of chores; they also were an endless task. We had to start all over again at the beginning of each row after we finally arrived at its end. The summer sun, good soil, and ample rain were their *Miracle Grow*, times three. There were no power clippers for us to use to keep those wildly propagating green monsters tidy. Only by manually opening and closing those clippers against the resistance of the new growth, with shears too big for our small and uncalloused hands, would the job get done. But there was a small riding, gas-powered lawnmower to cut the grass that loved to fecundly sprout again, as fast as we cut it, in the huge fields that flanked the hedges. Fields made for hitting a baseball or playing catch, but there was too little time and energy left to bother.

During the week, the mothers and the children (my sister, four cousins, and I) occupied and took care of the farm, which may be overstating our accomplishments. I dreaded Friday night when my uncle Ben would arrive. That was the crashing end to whatever dawdling and ice cream eating our mothers indulged us in during the week. Then, the work really began. My father stayed out of the way, being the smart guy he was. My uncle Ben had been a Navy officer and pilot instructor in World War II (defying many a Jewish stereotype at that time). I don't know, maybe he thought he was preparing my cousin and me for war. It seemed that way to me. What in the world beseeched this first-generation Jewish–American, from Queens, not Indiana, to fly warplanes and train other pilots, and then go about raising chickens? After a week of hard physical labor and small business worries at the autobody shop, how did he find the will—and energy—to drive deep up into New York's Hudson River Valley? To wake early the next day to tend a farm, not to mention run us boys into the ground?

Grumble as I may, the farm had rewards that amaze me to this day. When riding a horse down a steep mountain path or galloping in an arroyo I remember that I learned to ride—perhaps, more importantly, to be comfortable around those massive animals—in a corral down the road from the chicken farm. When I tried living in the country, before this city boy returned to the city, I knew how to plant and grow a garden, even knew how to deal with garden insects without pesticides. I knew how to build a fence to keep the deer and other scavengers away. I once surprised a French friend, a former commando who had served in Algeria, when I matched him in marksmanship with a rifle at his home in the Pyrenees. That was because I was prepared, trained: One of the high points of Walden was shooting a .22 rifle, at dusk, at an assortment of rusted cans placed at such distance that they were almost invisible against the backdrop of the ascending woods that framed the rear of the farm. I still can muster the smell of the bullets and the lubricant used to keep the guns in order.

More deeply, in ways a child cannot discern, at least not yet, I learned the ways by which family and community inter-depend. I witnessed how communal a group can be—must be—if it is to get the work of everyday life done. I saw leadership behavior in my uncle that was beyond the call of duty, as a pilot and a family man. I came to know my family not just as relations but as teachers and guides who were able to harness all our efforts together. To care for each other and transfer on the lessons about the basics of life, a tradition that traces back to our ancient, agrarian roots. I was stretched in ways (far beyond preparing me for scholastic aptitude tests) which then seemed to make no sense to me but became a basis for my forever straying beyond my comfort zone.

Which brings me to public service, my métier in government work, municipal and state, for near to two decades. While not unique to public service, cleaning up the residue left by others, however natural that may have been, is a part of the job. Often made more arduous by the cramped coop-like access from many a rule or regulation, and at the behest and for the sake of others. These are intrinsic not just to the job description but the duty it requires. Four years, eight, twelve, whatever the duration of an elected and appointed administration may be, the pruning and reshaping can never stop, since the hedges of public service have no horizon, no end in sight. The demands are endless, as well; and yes, they call for a lot of resolute work. The rewards of public service are there too, in ways that provide purpose, meaning, and community, as they did on the farm.

Walden was a crucible in my development. While I have had enough of yard work for this lifetime, I look forward to my next time on a horse or to confounding a person from the rural countryside or out west with my facility with a rifle. Back then, as well as now, I could feel pride in hard work consistently done, where actions, not words, are the only true measure. I have learned that rewards come in unexpected ways that may not be apparent for years to come.

In my childhood, drive and competency were the true commodities of exchange during the meritocracy often made possible in the fifties. I learned, too, that no one, especially children, dies from hard work, expectations, or responsibility. But mostly, I think, I learned that work never ends so I might as well find work of contribution, that I also love, since then it will feel to be a calling, and less like work.

*****

14A: Service

Service can connote what may be menial chores and duties. It also may have a luster of nobility, as when we think of soldiers and many other uniformed personnel, as well as the many others whose lives help ensure our safety. Clergy and missionaries have a long history of caring for the souls of others, often at great personal sacrifice (scandals by various churches notwithstanding). A calling often also is applied when considering the work of practicing doctors, nurses, public health workers (in the field, or in government and universities), teachers, and mothers and fathers, to name but a few vocations.

I have come to believe that a life well-lived, one of dignity instead of despair (thank you, Erik Erikson), must be earned. Mine is a perspective on life where meaning and contribution, our psychological oxygen, are not conferred upon us, nor purchased. It is a view where the most salient measure of my—of our—merit, of our moral selves, must be renewed again and again.

I am old enough and have had plenty of jobs. So students and trainees of all types are given to ask me: "What advice do you have for my career?"

I have said the same thing, for many years: "Find the hardest job you can (not an impossible job but a really hard

204

job), take it and master it. Then quickly search for your next job, which should be the hardest job you can find. Master that too, and then move on. And so on…"

The questioners that impress me the most are the ones that get it. Totally. They are seekers, pilgrims finding their way. They give me hope. They are the future we need.

In recent jobs I have had, I have overseen the work of a great many physicians (health professionals as well, but let me stay professionally local). I have had to recruit doctors for clinical work, administration, training, and research. Mostly for clinical and clinical administrative (like chiefs of service) posts. Turns out, in government and at not-for-profit hospitals (especially academic hospitals), the pay for psychiatrists does not match up to that of private practice, industry, and for-profit healthcare organizations. Mind you, it's not bad to be paid a six-figure amount—though its peanut butter may not cover the bread of college and university loans, apartments in high rent cities, private, elementary, high school or college tuitions for their children, a safe and roomy car for a growing family, even a nice holiday from time to time. Financial strain can and does happen even in two-income households.

But the recruiting is now better than ever, even for government psychiatrist jobs. Because when doctors are surveyed about "what matters most about your work?" pay does not top their ratings. What doctors seek, especially the next crop of them, are collegial relationships, a learning environment, being treated with respect (if they earn it), a decent work/life balance, the absence of onerous patient caseloads, shelter from the misery of dealing with managed care and insurance companies, limited on-call, and good benefits (health insurance principally, and retirement plans that optimize earnings and with employer contributions). Educational loan repayment programs are very helpful; did you know that the total amount of school loans in this country (all types of schools) is $1.8 trillion (yes, trillion) dollars, evidently inescapable by default, even bankruptcy? Geez.

Medicine is a calling. And it can feel more so the case if the doctor is not mired in the muck of insurance bureaucracy; or mindless and hugely time-consuming electronic medical record-keeping and insurance payment approvals; and a conveyer belt of patients where there is no time to listen, to understand, to provide useful guidance and support.

Public service, medical in this case, does not—should not—mean masochism. Government service (in settings free of moral bankruptcy and cynicism) also is a calling. Caring for other people, physically and psychologically (not just as a doctor) needs to be more of a calling if we are to successfully navigate the demands of an aging population. Caregiving, as well, may be an employment answer to the projections of how robots will kill most jobs in the future (mentioned in Chapter 1A). Farming should be considered a calling, perhaps not mega, industrialized agriculture— when we consider its endless demands (not just on the body) and its commercial and climate perils. The list should go on but sustaining your patience and attention span are the responsibilities of an author.

In ancient French, the word *servise* conveyed an act of homage; it evoked a sentiment I like since homage is paying respect to another. But its Latin root, *servitium*, demeans the action, making it closer to slavery—as *servus* means a slave. Its meaning went further downhill in the Middle Ages when service was meant as sexual intercourse. Matters improved when being a soldier (or sailor, airman/woman, Marine) became ennobling.

Service also can be in the eyes of the beholder. There is a wonderful parable about a man traveling along a path who comes upon two masons building a vast wall. The traveler asks, "What are you doing?" The first replies, "Breaking my back building this wall." The second replies, "Building a house for God."

In other words, we each may define what it means to be of service. But no matter how one may twist its meaning, it is not being of service when a position of power—like being a doctor, a member of the clergy, a public official, a law enforcement agent—is used not to give but to take. The media is redolent with examples, since their editors know the public has an appetite for seeing wrong taken to task, to shame the person who has violated our trust.

Sometimes it is an organization that has exploited its power, which has taken advantage of its necessary place in the lives of those dependent on it, like the pharmaceutical companies that have made life-sustaining or life-saving insulin or epinephrine injectable devices near to unaffordable. Or the banks that sold "derivatives" to pension funds and institutions, which were bundled mortgages (or other weak assets) that became portfolios of holdings without actual value. Or scientific labs and companies that defy the public trust when unashamedly claiming they have discovered diagnostic or genetic testing that reveals important medical information—when that is the fiction they have spun.

It has been said that an organization is the lengthened shadow of one man (sic). Behind each of the misanthropic organizational practices is a leader, or group of leaders, who fashioned a lie and calculated how to profiteer from its propagation. Why did no bankers go to prison after the 2008 financial meltdown? After their hedge fund trading of subprime mortgages led to the massive foreclosures that evicted so many families from their homes? That devastated many a future pension from which to live on when older? Those who spread, like a virus, a blend of toxic financial trading that sickened the global economy for almost a decade? Why do we see so many mendacious elected and appointed officials escape justice?

There are always people in essential and hugely influential positions who capitalize on our trust, our needs, and our money. The industrial and corporate titans that produce mayhem are not anonymous. They have leaders that disdain and dismiss their fiduciary responsibility. These are the bad guys that give so many others a bad name, who have induced the kind of cynicism that is rampant in our country, especially among youth and those economically and emotionally devastated by the malfeasance of some in power, who follow only their self-serving aims and their own rules.

Service is a calling, I believe. A cast of mind where contribution, giving something of value to others without seeking return or acclaim, is its defining dimension: service that is morally and ethically right – and, by contrast, that which is wrong. Where personal meaning and purpose, the pillars on which our lives are raised high, by which we best judge ourselves, derive from doing good, in ways small and large, day after day. Not with any pretense or pretext of being special, but with humility. That's what makes for a true, not a faux, public servant.

It was Pope Francis who called for "…small acts of kindness, not great speeches…" That man has said so many things right and lives a life consonant with his words.

*****

Concluding Thoughts

What Matters?

This book looks back more than 65 years in my life. Its boundaries in time are from my latency age as a boy until I went off to college. I thought it would strain—likely be beyond—my imagination to dredge up my early years. Yet when I sat down, keyboard at my fingertips, out poured all these memories. This set of 14 stories, each clear and full in my head, but with no true warrant on the truth. Nor are there a gaggle of witnesses to such an unnoticed early life, only a few remaining family members. These tales, thus, may be more like wistful musings, about my past and about what matters, than literal facts. But they are my memories, as best as I can convey them. At least what I have discovered over a long period of time.

While, of course, the facts usually matter, our memories are riddled with errors from the erosion of time and the way our brain fixes remembrances into its circuitry. A crucial brain memory center, the hippocampus, is highly subject to the amygdala, where our feelings are activated. We thus mostly remember what is salient, of emotional valence. And even then, those traces of the past are further morphed and condensed with others and collected through the years—

subject to the distortions, not necessarily of volition, intrinsic to the human mind. So, my stories are just that: a ménage of fact, fiction, and the liberty of a creative process. They are not a history book (as if that were picture-perfect).

Yet it is not the factualness or literalness of any tale that evokes its meaning; it is what we make of the story in our mind's eye. Meaning, in other words, is a product of the complex interplay of person, family, culture, and circumstances. These are akin to the notes, cadences, and harmonies that make up the musical score that constitutes our mind. And, they are usually anchored in the era from which they were born. Therein lie the threads that weave our tales. While these here are only my stories, and riffs on them, of course, I hope that they may echo or resonate with yours, as well as many others, yesterday and today.

As I spun my stories onto a computer screen, I came upon unexpected and curious doors that begged to be opened, to be given further consideration. Perspectives, if you will, on the ideas and themes that are the fabric, the whole, of the stories. Hence, I wrote essays paired with each of the stories. These are my way of trying to understand, by way of exposition, more about me (and my fellow human beings) and the world I lived in. I wanted to have each tale furthered and colored by its time in history, its culturally bound dimensions, family (of course), the humor and pathos of everyday life, about growing up and growing older, and about what really matters.

Work

Take, for example, the essay that accompanies the lead story, *Ink-Stained for Life.* There is the old saw that no one on (usually his, not her) deathbed wishes for more time at work. The regrets are usually about time not spent with family, friends, engaged in pleasure (innocent and carnal), creative pursuits, and meaningful contribution. But I don't know. I love work, have all my life.

For me, work—and mine does not break my back, callus my hands, or numb my mind with endless repetition, no small matters—has always been a rich source of meaning and purpose. Sure, I am a doctor. I have trained to be one since my 20s and practiced for many decades. Medical school and residency were demanding endeavors but matched by the fascination of the science and the wonder of body and mind, of the special privilege that service to others provides, and, after medical school, a steady income and reliable employment (though, as mentioned, not quite sufficient compensation for those bearing a vast educational debt). I believe that medical school should be tuition-free but with commensurate public service due upon graduation.

I know that some in my profession may principally feel its burdens and anxieties; after all, we are trying to keep people alive and at good levels of functioning. There is the bureaucratic labor too; especially, the time in a day spent more on charting and "paperwork," which can now typically be more than with patients. I know too, as a psychiatrist, the significant prevalence of depression and substance use among my colleagues—and the horrifically common death by suicide among doctors in training and in practice. These are preventable tragedies. I say so not just because that is what I do for a living. But it will take some considerable doing to support a culture of self-care and seeking help among physicians that will make a significant, needed, salubrious difference in their lives.

Some feel a diminution in status: the doctor no longer "knows best." Yet, as we are rid of that past illusion, my profession is beginning to experience the pleasure of working in teams, and in sharing dilemmas and decisions with patients and their families (when possible), and of course colleagues. If we step back a bit, sometimes we even can feel the calling of our work, how we are graced to be able to serve.

I had no idea about all this stuff when in my early years. But something began to happen in my teenage brain, in high school. I had gained entrance through an exam to a public high school that fully worked my brain and mind, more so than any other time in my life. It was a school that set very high bars (not in sports!) and had a good share of inspirational teachers. I felt the pull of education and knowledge, of trying to master complex matters like physics, science, and even the proper use of the English language. I still have that feeling.

I feel fortunate, grateful throughout my professional life, for having been able to do well at caring for patients and their families. For having the privilege of teaching, early and ongoing, so I could nurture the generation of doctors to come. And later on, being able to shape and work to improve mental health policy and clinical practice. I started writing early in my career, as a resident; it was then and still is in my bones. I was ambitious and able, and climbed my professional ladder, landing some of the best jobs in my field. But I was not born on third base; I had to earn each base in order to score.

What happens inside me when I am working at what I love? Time seems to disappear. Aches and pains recede. Focus replaces mental abandonment and listlessness. Many times, hopefully, the product of the work helps someone else: could be a patient, a family member, a student, a colleague, a member of the lay public who has read something I wrote or an audio or video I recorded, and when I do a valued service in (or for) an honorable institution or professional organization. There is, as well, the inestimable experience of contribution, living outside of myself, in the service of others. The feeling of being of use, having purpose during the brief time I am blessed to be alive.

I don't think a person needs to be a doctor to like work. Nor even be another professional, like a teacher, nurse, attorney, a member of the uniformed services (military, police, firefighters, EMTs, and the like), a business(wo)man, and so on. Artists, musicians, dancers, filmmakers, and other artisans of all stripes are just as much professionals, but in the creative arts. Athletes too. When I was young, the only life I wanted, dreamed of, more than becoming a pro basketball player (like Bill Bradley) was to be a dancer. These were childhood dreams since I had not a whiff of understanding the skills needed.

Labor itself can have its satisfactions. There are technical skills, achieved by training, like fixing something broken, building or creating something, cooking, caring for someone, and so on. There is the pride of work well done. I hope my plumber and electrician think so, because they make my life better, and deserve to feel that way. And there are the massive number of public servants who make my water pure, my air breathable, and my streets and roads safe and clean. Thank you, for what seldom receives gratitude.

A larger field of vision

Some say we are in a dark time. Climate change; the center of families and communities no longer holding; the risk of the erosion of the inestimable importance of American democracy; ever-growing health and wealth disparities; political and citizen divisiveness; the opioid and the loneliness epidemics (the latter conferring the same health risk as smoking 15 cigarettes/day, the former deadlier than the HIV/AIDS epidemic at its apogee and with a death toll greater than the Vietnam War); leaving more of the mentally disabled without a safety net—left to endure the miseries of living on the streets and in jails and prisons. And in 2020, the global coronavirus pandemic. You can add to the list…

Over 100 years ago, the French sociologist Émile Durkheim created the term *anomie*, without a name, being non-persons, and attributed the condition to instilling the wish to die by suicide—is this the sum of these dark parts?

Yet, paradoxically, from a historical and public health perspective, the world is doing better (perhaps not the United States—see Appendix A). A billion people globally have been relieved of starvation. People live longer. There are far fewer children and mothers lost in childbirth. We generally have (leaving out huge segments of slums in underdeveloped countries) vastly improved sanitation and highly effective vaccinations, and had better control of what were deadly or crippling infectious illnesses (though COVID's legacy is not looking good). Almost everyone has a cell phone; some might question its value, but it is the magical connection to others, to information, and to safety.

But... but—to paraphrase a phrase from my brilliant colleagues, Drs. Richard Frank and Sherry Glied—we are *better but far from well*. Besides, happiness experts tell us it's all relative anyway. Every improvement spawns the yearning for another. A great many today cannot imagine life without a source of power, a refrigerator, transportation, a TV, even some modicum of education. Each step up the ladder, paradoxically, satisfies us yet it *also* spawns the expectation for more—which, itself, can leave us feeling unfulfilled.

Indeed. But we have today's problems, not those of the mid-19th century or, God forbid, the Middle Ages. Still, the persistent and vast gulf between the haves and the have nots has made basic human rights like housing, healthcare, food security, education, and safety elusive for far too many people. Those legions who live in the big shadow cast by "the 1%." Those in our country left in that pall have grown in number and now span all races and ethnicities (though Black Americans have been the most profoundly denied in the US). Obvious disparities have a way of producing enmity, when, for example, Watts borders on Beverly Hills, LA, and Park Slope with Bed-Stuy, Brooklyn. It is a surprise that more riots have not erupted. To make matters worse, the bitterness of being on the wrong side of the divide, left behind in the land of opportunity, has become grist for mills of politicians who trade in blame and hate.

We are, to risk repetition, better but far from well. And what matters to each of us is how far from well, in its myriad of dimensions, we and our family are today, not how we might have felt 100 or 1,000 years ago.

Wisdom

I wish I could confidently say what wisdom is. Lacking that capacity, I believe I know what it is not: Being self-absorbed, so that the humanity and suffering about us has become invisible. It is bigotry, racism, and palpable or subtle (death by a thousand indignities) discrimination. It is injustice, allowing for the denial of basic human rights, including fairness (equity), freedom, health and education, housing, and food on the table. These are the foundations of the social good that a wise person should support.

But does it only take a wise person to know these? Or might another person not see what may be hidden in plain sight? Like those blindfolded by their despair and disappearing prospects for a decent life for themselves—and their progeny. The circumstances, the realities, that breed fear and anger, that preoccupy some on the short end of the societal stick. That foster a restive society that has lost the plot of equity and loving thy neighbor, of "brotherly" love.

Wisdom is not just knowing a lot of things. You might win on *Jeopardy* but not succeed in having a good or decent life. It seems that having the quotidian experiences of personal and social safety, of equal opportunity, and of a figuratively "colorblind" society is usually necessary to know and live by what is most important: namely, that which is humane and fair. But it is really hard to climb up the moral hierarchy if every day your stomach cries out for food and your body for shelter.

Values

If I was frightless enough to take on wisdom, I might as well go ahead with the subject of values. These, we may be fortunate to appreciate, are the essential, fundamental, beliefs we each can hold dear and tight. The principles that guide our moral compass and our behaviors.

They are not what Groucho Marx famously said: *Those are my principles, and if you don't like them… well, I have others.*

Core values include loyalty; fairness (the "Golden Rule"); being honest, trustworthy, and dependable; respecting others and the limited resources of our planet; striving for excellence or simply to be as able as we can be; faith (more about this below); perhaps being driven to seek solutions, rather than to usher in blame or cry out in defeat.

I suspect values may add up to knowing right from wrong, responsibility from indifference, and kindness (I love the French expression: Vous étés très gentil[le]) As a psychiatrist, I imagine values are instilled from witnessing others, who are close or respected, who exercise these principles in everyday life. Values do not seem to me simply didactically acquirable. They may be more like, see one, do one, teach one (even if that also is a popular motto in medical education).

Family

We all know the joke, "You can choose your friends but you can't choose your family." Its ubiquity in human social discourse must say a lot.

Perhaps one of the greatest and solvable public health problems we face in our country are what have been termed

"ACEs": Adverse Childhood Experiences. Over 20 years ago, in Northern California, a study of adults looking back on their childhood years was undertaken by Kaiser Permanente, in collaboration with the Centers for Disease Control and Prevention (CDC). This work lifted the veil off the view that childhood usually is both a walk in the park and, other than infectious and hereditary diseases, not a period that bred future illness and despair.

The researchers queried not inner-city people of color living in poverty but the middle-class subscribers to Kaiser, an HMO (Health Maintenance Organization). They asked about the traumas in their early lives. As you might imagine, even with the stunning findings of trauma in the samples of people they surveyed, poverty and discrimination amplify the production of ACEs.

ACEs include physical, verbal, and sexual abuse; physical and emotional neglect; untreated and active addiction and mental illness in the home; being witness to domestic violence; having a parent or guardian incarcerated; and living in multiple foster homes. The researchers called each of these an ACE, giving the value of one point to each one, so they could be summed. They frequently co-occurred adding to the total number of ACEs a child might have experienced.

Over many years and many studies, the higher the number of ACEs reported (usually five or more), the stronger the predictive value of later having problems of drug abuse and violence to the self or other. Other, less valent but no less important, consequences of high ACE scores included developing, as early as in adolescence, obesity (and the early stages of diabetes); depression;

trouble with the law; teenage pregnancy; and early onset of smoking.

The reality of early childhood trauma is now undisputed. But its substantial presence and impact on the health and well-being of many children (more than we care to imagine) is not commensurate with programs for the preventative delivery of parental skill-building, of the treatment of active mental and substance use disorders in families, and containing the unbridled use of the criminal justice system for non-violent behaviors and as an "answer" to the societal problems of untreated, serious mental and addictive disorders.

One thing I have learned from leading large, mental health responses to human-made and natural disasters (including 9/11 in NYC, Hurricane Sandy, and others) is how *resilient* we humans are. Resilience, the intrinsic or acquired capacity to recover despite disaster and misfortune, is the silver lining of trauma. It is why some who suffer profound trauma, in childhood, war, forced immigration, and the like, do better than others. Some of the predictors of resilience we have seen in the wake of disasters include supportive families, trusted friends, cohesive communities, and faith (more about this below). Those are the qualities to uncover and support in those whose lives have been upended by trauma—no matter what may be its cause.

There are so many of us—me included—who have been spared childhood (or adult) trauma. We come from families that may have our share of burdens, conflicts, and defeats yet who also bestowed the experience of attachment, and nurtured aspirations, appreciated successes and kindled hope. These are families who did not unleash their emotional pain in the ways that produce ACEs.

My parents were both first-generation, Jewish–American New Yorkers. They set out to raise their kids to have more than they did, to prosper themselves through the business(es) they built, and to acculturate.

What does it mean to acculturate? It is a pervasive drive, I suppose, in immigrants and their progeny. For my parents, both with only high-school educations, that meant running a small business and trying to generate an ever-increasing standard of living. To assure their children were educated, at a good college (when my sister and I were young, our parents did not know from graduate school—except becoming a doctor or a lawyer). To follow a Jewish ethnicity, if not religion. To have a home, a nice (read expensive) car, and to look and behave a bit like the Gentiles; not the Irish or Italians, but the WASPS. As for me, you can pick me out in a crowd. I look like a Jewish psychiatrist from central casting, except I don't have on a cardigan or corduroy pants.

I seem to have gone on a long time here about family. I hope you take that as a measure of the gold therein. The ways, good and awful, a family behaves and the inescapability of its role in who we are and aspire to be. I can tell you, it's much easier (and more fun) to be a grandparent than a parent. I have learned from my son, my wife, and a few special guides in my life that gratitude enriches our souls and our lives. This section, thus ends, with my unequivocal gratitude for my family, with its pilgrimage from Eastern Europe to America and by the four generations I have been blessed to know.

A Spiritual Life, a Life Marked by Faith

I asked, in a published interview I did of a good friend and colleague of mine, Paul Summergrad, MD,—who had the same job I did at MGH but went on to be an academic, department Chair at Tufts and the President of the American Psychiatric Association (neither of which have I achieved, nor will)—how he thought of spirituality? He had provided these thoughts at a talk at a national psychiatric meeting, thus my query.

He remarked, "Spirituality is linked to a sense of meaning, purpose, ineffability, or (potentially) experiences of unity with the world, even grace. While religious experiences may include all of these elements, religions are often viewed as a specific set of beliefs, often within a ritual or communal canon, including accompanying texts and ordained clergy."

Perhaps I should stop here? There is so much he packs into his response. You may want to reread it.

But I can't, won't, because I should take a crack at the same.

When asked, I say I am a spiritual person, but hold to no religion, though I do have a palpable Jewish ethnicity, flavored by being a New Yorker. What I am trying to convey, like many others I know, is that I believe in a "higher power," not a God-head, but an unimaginable, undefinable, more than enormous, and pervasive force. One that is both creative and destructive, because nature encompasses both life and death. I have no rituals to anchor my view. You might say I have science to back me up, in light of what we have come to know of our solar system and its minuscule place in the universe. About how time and space interdigitate, as Einstein proposed. How mass and energy are merely different expressions of the same phenomenon if that is what it is. All indicia, I imagine, of this force and power.

The scale, munificence, ineffability, and wonder that scientific discovery has revealed so far are daunting to me. And science has barely penetrated the real and figurative black holes of what has yet to be discerned. I cannot get my head around the dimensions, no less the power that shapes everything. Power not over just me, us, but everything *around* us, near and very, very far. About everything *about* us, matter and mind. There is more going on here than I can divine, even if it is not literally divine. And that leads me to think further on the forces we can witness, which may seem random to some, but I can't buy that. There feels to be something preternatural going on, beyond the limits of our vision. And I am not given to conspiracy theories.

I also have felt, over many years and in different ways, the presence of those forces. Their immanence in all that abounds about us: the fertile earth, the life-giving rain, the fury of the seas, and all living things—plants, animals, birds, and fish (amphibians too), insects, bacteria, viruses, and so on, including what we have yet to be able to witness. This view I espouse that God is immanent is held by many religious leaders I have met.

One moment I like to report (I can send you the photo I took at the time if you wish) happened not many years ago. Over 10 years, my wife and I walked (and completed) an ancient pilgrimage trail. It extends 1,600 kilometers from south-central France, south to and over the Pyrenees on the Napoleon trail, then heads due west, in Northern Spain. The

Santiago de Compostelle Pilgrimage Trail (the Way of St. Jacques/Saint James), which ends literally in the city that bears its name. Though a pilgrim comes to understand that the trail, Le Voie in French, The Way in English, El Camino in Spanish, never ends. We were near Pamplona. The going had been awful that morning: heavy winds, horizontal rain, a violent hailstorm (a bit Biblical, I admit). We were beaten down, soaked, even to our socks and boots. Then the vengeful weather suddenly stopped. Rosanne, my wife, said, "Look behind you!" There was a full rainbow, stunning in its glory. We were witnessing that morning what often is offered as a metaphor for the trials we face: where bearing up to whatever besets us on our path may be, can be sometimes, followed by a glorious moment, one of awe. Beauty has been portrayed for us if we can turn and see the light.

Other experiences of the presence of the hand of something like a god have occupied my dream life for a very long time. My nocturnal mind has been to distant and strange places, conjured up images and physical experiences that have rattled me. For a very long time, I have had what are called "lucid dreams," not only exceptionally vivid but allowing a conscious experience to co-exist with a dream. There are books about lucid dreaming. I critically reviewed one a long time ago because it romanticized this form of dreaming, urged readers to learn how to have or increase their lucid dreams. For me, these are haunting, high-speed dysphoric states that I have learned to control (a bit), not wondrous adventures. Yet they too add to my sense that so much more is going on—and that dream states can touch the beyond.

I have been able, a few times, to feel the pain of someone personally close yet physically far away, and to verify those experiences when I could. I have beheld the utter wonder of birth, and the last breaths and then the peace of death in family members and patients. I have come upon the immanence of a higher power countless times when mindful about what I am seeing on the earth and skies above. I have come to believe in a higher power, without believing in God. This is no humbug, as was said a long time ago about the wonder of ether as a surgical anesthetic.

Faith seems to me to be another matter. I don't have a lot of faith. When things don't go well, I typically expect a bad outcome. That is not faith, that is lacking in faith. My wife, a practicing Catholic, has faith. She is sanguine when trouble enters her field of vision. Not unrealistic, but bearing a faith that what is happening is fundamentally ordained, and will work itself out—especially if we aide in the process. I envy her faith. I don't know how to acquire it. So far, I have not found a religious path to provide it.

In some ways, lacking faith may have influenced my choice of and practice of medicine. Medical school, for me, was gathering information that could serve, even quell, my uncertainty. My medical school and residency training, followed by years of practicing psychiatry and public health, have made me more attentive, full of worry about my patients and the errors and neglects that can befall them. I am not one to take anything for granted. Yet, I would like to have faith. I think I would suffer less.

A memoir is to a significant extent a vanity project. Especially when the author has not changed the course of the river, so to speak. I have worked to do my part in making things a little better, day by day, in both my professional and personal lives. I am proud of my contributions. Of the stories that depict moments in my life. But who would care to read about them, save a handful of family and friends?

The question is empirical. The answer lies in putting this manuscript out there to see what happens.

*****

Appendix A

How are we doing as a country when it comes to health?

Sargent Joe Friday, the indomitable detective of the great 1950s TV series, *Dragnet*, gave us the expression, "All we want are the facts, ma'am," of which became the trope, "Just the facts, ma'am."

So, let's start with some facts, before we return to my meanderings, brought to us by *The National Center for Health Statistics*, in its report on *Health, United States, 2017.* (https://www.cdc.gov/nchs/hus/index.htm). Italics are mine.

- 2015 marked the *first significant decrease in life expectancy* since 1993, which has continued into 2016.
- The troubling shortening of lives in this country is primarily due to *drug overdose, suicide, and chronic liver disease (often a consequence of a substance use disorder).*
- *Drug overdose deaths increased by* 72% between 2006 and 2016.

- *Death by suicide increased* from 11.0 to 13.5 deaths per 100,000 (population).
- Among the ten most common preventable causes of death, *suicide is the only one that continues to rise.*
- *Deaths from chronic liver disease, including alcohol and drug-related cirrhosis, increased* by 5.3% per year, from 2012–2016, after no changes in the preceding six years.
- During this same period, the greatest increases in death rates were among *men and women aged 25–34.*
- What has *not* changed are the *leading causes of death* for the entire population, which are unintentional injuries in those aged 1–44, and for those older, it is heart disease and cancer.

The Princeton economists, Anne Case and Sir Angus Deaton, have portrayed the reduction in American lifespans, especially among middle-aged white men without college educations, to be "deaths by despair." These are people in the USA being left behind: jobless, with few prospects for their future or that of their children. They often suffer chronic pain from a life of manual labor and employ opioids and alcohol to relieve their physical and mental pain. Hopelessness and depression are common co-travelers, adding to the increase in deaths by suicide.

This demographic for deaths of despair is also spreading to millennials, aged 18–34, in the USA. A recent report from the UK suggests that this deadly trend is appearing there as well, though more evident there in middle-aged men.

These "facts" are not *fake news*. They are warning signs that growing segments of our country are losing faith in the future. These are people feeling agonizingly trapped in a downward spiral of disappearing opportunity and hope. They thus bathe themselves in substances that transport them away from the pain of their quotidian lives.

The *health gap* between the haves (with a whole lot) and the have-nots has grown from 1993 to 2017. The Centers for Disease Control and Prevention (CDC)—using its continuously updated seven categories of financial status—reports (2019) that a survey of how individuals with *wealth assess their health remains the same*; in other words, it has not changed in 25 years. But the assessment of the *health of low-income people has changed "substantially."*

Health "equity," the just and fair opportunity to feel well, is not improving. For our country, which spends more money on medical care per capita than any other in the world, we are not doing well enough. Here the facts suggest that we are not only *not* getting better, but we are also growing the health gap between rich and poor. Aside from the moral arguments that need to apply when this happens, it spawns unrest and divisiveness, individually, locally, and nationally. (JAMA Network Open. 2019;2(6):e196386. doi:10.1001/jamanetworkopen.2019.6386).

There is much rhetoric about closing these gaps. About beating the unchecked epidemics of substance disorders (especially opioids, with crystal methedrine on the rise) and deaths by suicide. About health inequities. About supplying treatment instead of incarceration.

Complex problems like these require comprehensive and enduring approaches. These wed public health with interventions that aim to mitigate what has now come to be called the "social determinants" of health, including poverty, housing, education, food insecurity, work opportunity, and a livable wage.

There is reason to hope. There are cities, counties, and even some states bringing together their intelligence and will to identify particular problems and what works for their remediation. They are defying the continued support of established business and organizational (self) interests that feed on existing problems and aver or dismiss demonstrable solutions. These towns and states employ the prudent use of existing resources – money, real-estate, preventable health expenditures, for example – which can be repurposed to be more effective in achieving the social good. And who use real-time and on-going performance metrics that are reliably measured so they can't be gamed. These are communities exercising a relentless and iron will.

I offer my rays of hope not as a writer but as a public health doctor. I have spent the last 18 years in government roles working to produce results, a bit at a time, and I know so many others are doing the same, and more. We are not yet at a tipping point, that's clear. We are still slipping. I pray that even more agony and waste not be needed to catalyze essential changes and truly quiet the unrest that inhabits so many persons and communities.

*****